THE DESCENDANTS OF

ANTHONY LECLAR

ANTHONY LECLAR
1782-1869

THE DESCENDANTS OF

ANTHONY LECLAR

(of Oneida County, New York)

1782 - 1869

Compiler & Editor : Robert G. Yorks

Compiler : Audra Minnie (Meeker) LeClar

South Oxford Press
Oxford, NY 13830
2010

Library of Congress Control Number: 2010922503

Published by
South Oxford Press
2139 County Road 3
Oxford, NY 13830
607-843-5629
southoxfordpress@live.com

INTRODUCTION

This genealogy was initiated by a friend, Jerry LeClar, asking a simple question about a name found in an 1875 Atlas of Oneida County, NY. That name was M. LeClar and Jerry wanted to know who it was and if he, Jerry, was related to this M. LeClar.

One thing led to another and I soon found myself with a file of LeClar family data. Being an inquisitive sort, I started putting the data together and this is what we have. And, yes, Jerry is related to the M. LeClar (Moulton) whose name is in the Atlas.

I did find, also, that there are many other branches to this family tree. Anthony LeClar and his descendants are only one small branch of a much larger family tree. There appears to be a lot of data for this greater family already gathered in several places, so I may try to compile it all into one coherent family genealogy at some time in the future.

Understand also that there are and have been numerous versions of the spelling of this family's name, and that that is not unusual for families with names that lend themselves to misunderstanding or to alternative spellings. Some of the names are: Clear, Cleer, LeClair, LeClaire, LeClear, LeCleer, and LeClerc which also occur with the C not connected as in Le Clar, plus misspellings in many of the census records such as LaClear, Laleer, Lclear, Lablear, and on-and-on. The most common alternative spellings appears to be LeClair and LeClear.

i

The father of Anthony LeClar, in all probability, was John Clear, who was in Oneida County about 1794 in the Town now known as Western near the location of what would become the Village of North Western. Two older histories, *Our County and Its People: A Descriptive Work on Oneida County, New York*, edited by Daniel E. Wager (1896); and the *History of Oneida County, New York, 1667 – 1878*, by Samuel W. Durant (1878), give this account:

The first permanent settler on the site of the village (North Western) was David Utley, from Columbia Co., N.Y., who located here about 1794-95, and purchased two hundred acres of land. On the portion of this place now occupied by his son, Squire Utley, a man named John Clear had "squatted", built a small log house, and made a clearing. He had been here about a year when Mr. Utley arrived. The latter allowed him to keep fifty acres, but afterwards purchased it of him.. Clear had no title in the first place, and Mr. Utley consented to his remaining in order that he might get a start in the world, and not have the work he had already done go for naught.

Although these histories mention John Clear, they do not mention his family which in 1794 consisted of a wife and ten children, seven boys and three girls, all born in New York before 1794, so it would appear that he had a lot of help clearing the land when he arrived in Oneida County. There is another history of the county which also mentions Baptista LeClar in Western, Oneida County, NY in the 1790s. Baptista was a son of John Clear and an older brother to Anthony LeClar.

It is reported that John Clear was born in 1740 in France as Jean LeClerc. What is not clear, yet, is when he came to this country and when and where he married Jane Taylor. There is some family 'lore' that says that he came in 1777 with General Lafayette, but that seems very unlikely. That would mean that the first seven children were born in France and it appears that there are U.S. records that support most of the children being born in the U.S. One son, Peter (1769-1862) says in both the 1850 and 1860 U.S. censuses that he was born in New York. So I think we can assume that Jean/John came to the U.S. early in life, perhaps as a young man and married here.

It is believed that Jean LeClerc's parents were Baptista (1706) and Abigale (1709). His ancestry before that gets even hazier, but the general trail may go back through Baptista and Abigale, then (through a missing link) to a Jean Baptiste Leclerc (1640-1693), and lastly to a Francois Leclercq (1608-1679) and Genevieve St. Michel (????-1685) in Faches, Nord, Nord-Pas-de-Calais, France, which is in Northern France near Calais and Dunkirk.

At the end of this book there is a descendant chart which shows what the early family looked like with these early French persons as ancestors of this American LeClar family.

Anyone having additions or corrections they would like to have considered may forward them to me at one of the addresses on the copyright page. If enough changes are warranted, I will publish a second edition and alert everyone who has a copy of this edition.

There are several people to thank for their contributions to this work, including Jerry & Gerry LeClar, Dick and Joyce LeClar, Pete & Annie Cummings and Linda Kay (Fine) Lawrence.

However, without the personal manuscript of one person, this work would have been a lot shorter. A major contribution to the family names, dates, pictures and newspaper articles has been made to this publication by the posthumous papers of AUDRA MINNIE (MEEKER) LECLAR. Copies of some her manuscripts have been graciously made available to me by Audra's family and because of the significance of this data, and the desire to publicly recognize her work, Audra's name is not only on the title page of this book, but also on the back cover. Given more time, Audra would have produced this book herself.

Respectfully submitted to the LeClar Family with the warmest regards to my friends Jerry and Dick LeClar.

Robert G. Yorks
April, 2010

Gerald Allen LeClar
(1949 -   )

Harold Richard LeClar
(1942 -   )

Descendants of Anthony LeClar

Generation No. 1

1. ANTHONY[1] LECLAR was born 1782 in Dutchess County, NY?, and died 1869 in Western, Oneida County, NY. He married c1807, MARTHA HAYNES. She was born Sep 1788[1], and died 03 Jul 1858 in Western, Oneida County, NY[2].

ANTHONY and MARTHA are buried in the Frenchville Cemetery, Western, Oneida County, NY

Children of ANTHONY LECLAR and MARTHA HAYNES are:
2.   i.   JOHN BATTIS[3] LECLAR, b. 21 May 1808, Western, Oneida County, NY; d. 30 Jan 1864, Western, Oneida County, NY.
     ii.   SOLOMON LECLAR, b. Bet. 1811 - 1812, Western, Oneida County, New York[3]; d. 08 Jul 1885, New York City, NY[4]. He is buried in the Frenchville Cemetery, Western, Oneida County, NY. Never married.

Rome Sentinel July 16, 1885
Ava - News has been received here of the death of Solomon LeClar, of Ava, which occurred in New York City. Mr. LeClar started on July 2 for New York with a lot of oars. On the morning of July 4 he was found sitting on a curbstone at the office of John T. Smith, an old friend of his, on South Street. He was taken in and cared for, and later was removed to the hospital where he died of typhoid congestion on Wednesday morning, July 8, age 74 years. His sister, Mrs. Charles Reynolds, was notified at once, and a brother of the deceased went to bring the remains here for interment. The funeral services will occur today at the Webster Hill Welsh Church. The deceased formerly lived in Western and later in Ava. Three sisters and one brother survive.

iii. PETER LECLAR, b. Bet. 1813 - 1814, Western, Oneida County, New York; d. Aft. 05 Jun 1880, California (prob.)[5]. PETER LECLAR is shown in both the 1860 and the 1880 censuses, in California, in two different but close locations, but no record has been found for him in either the 1870 census or for Civil War involvement.

In 1860 PETER is living in Angels Falls, Township #8, Calaveras County, California and working as a miner. This was a gold mining area and had residents from as far away as China mining for gold.

In 1880 PETER is living in San Joaquin in the near-bye county of Stanislaus and is recorded as a farmer.

There is no record of his ever marrying or of a wife and children.

Peter LeClar

3. iv. MARY A. LECLAR, b. Bet. Jan - Apr 1816, Western, Oneida County, NY; d. 03 Apr 1892, Western, Oneida County, NY.

4. v. SARAH LECLAR, b. 14 Jul 1822, Western, Oneida County, NY; d. 1915.

5. vi. JANE LECLAR, b. 14 Jul 1822, Western, Oneida County, NY; d. 31 Oct 1894, Leominster, Worcester, MA..

vii. MOULTON LECLAR, b. Oct 1828, Western, Oneida County, NY[7,8]; d. 07 Feb 1908, Western, Oneida County, NY[9]. He is buried in the Frenchville Cemetery in Western, Oneida County, NY. He never married.

Rome Sentinel February 8, 1908

Boonville - Moulton LeClare, who resides a short distance from this place, was found Thursday morning by neighbors lying on the floor of his home. Mr. LeClare was 79 years old and lived alone in a small house on the Ava Road. Although unconscious, he was still alive, but he expired in a short time, before the arrival of a physician. Coroner Moorey of Remsen was sent for and with Dr. Bartlett of Boonville viewed the remains. The cause of death was apoplexy. The remains were taken to the home of his sister, Mrs. Reynolds of Ava.

Rome Sentinel February 9, 1908

Ava - Mrs. Sarah Reynolds was greatly shocked to hear of the death of her only brother, Moulton LeClair, who was found by a neighbor in a dying condition. "Uncle Moult" as he was called, lived by himself in a small house just in the edge of Western, near Flint Town. Three years ago he spent the winter with his sister, Mrs. Reynolds, who would gladly have had him remain if he would, but he preferred to live by himself. Uncle Moult followed surveying until old age and rheumatism compelled him to give it up. Funeral services were held at the home of his sister on Saturday afternoon and interment was made in Wells Cemetery.

Moulton LeClar is mentioned in the 1875 Atlas of Oneida County as a surveyor.

Rebecca Webster LeClar
1812 - 1891

Generation No. 2

2. JOHN BATTIS[2] LECLAR *(ANTHONY[1])* was born 21 May 1808 in Western, Oneida County, NY[10], and died 30 Jan 1864 in Western, Oneida County, NY[11]. He married, May 1833 in Western, Oneida County, NY, REBECCA WEBSTER, daughter of ASA WEBSTER and ELIZABETH DOUGLASS. She was born 21 May 1812 in Western, Oneida County, New York, and died 16 Sep 1891 in Rome, Oneida County, NY. In the 1840 census JOHN's name is recorded as JOHN P. CLAR, in the 1850 census as 'JOHN CLEER', and in the 1860 census it is 'JOHN B. Le CLARE' and his widow is recorded as 'REBECCA LALLEAR' in the 1870 census.

Both JOHN and REBECCA are buried in the Frenchville Cemetery, Western, Oneida County, NY REBECCA's Tombstone Inscription: *Wife of John B. LeClar, age 79 yrs 3 mos 25 dys*

Rome Sentinel September 17, 1891
Mrs. Rebecca LeClar, widow of John B. LeClar, died at her home, 409 West Park Street, at 11:30 pm Wednesday, in he 80th year. She had been an invalid for several years, with a complication of diseases. The deceased was a daughter of the late Asa Webster of Webster Hill, in the town of Western, where she was born. She had lived in Rome about 16 years. She previously resided in Ava, where her husband died 26 years ago. She was a woman of broad intelligence, genial presence and charitable disposition. She was a member of the Wesleyan Methodist Church. She leaves surviving her a daughter, the wife of Rev. Robert Flint of Black river, NY, a son, Peter LeClar of Whitehouse, Ohio, a sister, Mrs. Esther Owens of Ava, and two brothers, Caleb Webster of Elkhorn, Wis., and Albert Webster of Western. Daughter of Asa and Elizabeth Douglass Webster

Children of JOHN LECLAR and REBECCA WEBSTER are:

      i.   ASA WEBSTER[3] LECLAR, b. Jul 1834, Western, Oneida County, New York; d. Sep 1834.

6.   ii. FERDINAND LECLAR, b. 01 Mar 1836, Western, Oneida County, NY; d. 30 Mar 1882, Western, Oneida County, NY.

7.   iii. MARY ANN LECLAR, b. 30 Jan 1839, Western, Oneida County, New York; d. 12 Jan 1913, Black River, Jefferson County, NY.

8.   iv. ELIZABETH LECLAR, b. 1841, Western, Oneida County, New York.

       v.   FLORETTA LOUISA LECLAR[12], b. 1847, Western, Oneida County, New York[13]; d. 15 Jan 1883, Knoxboro, NY. Never married. Floretta is buried in Rome Cemetery, Rome, Oneida County, NY. plot: Section H Lot 110

9.   vi. PETER B. LECLAR, b. Nov 1849, Western, Oneida County, New York; d. 09 Mar 1917, Jeffersonville, Fayette County, Ohio.

ADIN BUTLER

3. MARY ANN² LECLAR *(ANTHONY¹)* was born Bet. Jan - Apr 1816 in Western, Oneida County, NY, and died 03 Apr 1892 in Western, Oneida County, NY. She married, 06 Jan 1839 in Western, Oneida County, NY, ADIN H. BUTLER, son of JOSEPH BUTLER and POLLY SCOVIL. He was born Jan 1812 in Jefferson County, NY, and died 09 Jul 1895 in Ava, Oneida, NY¹⁴.

Both MARY and ADIN are buried in the Frenchville Cemetery in Western, Oneida County, NY. Her tombstone inscription is: *Wife of Adin H. Butler, age 76 yrs*

Rome Sentinel April 4, 1892
Mrs. Mary A. Butler, wife of Adin H. Butler, died of the grip at her home, 419 West Liberty Street, on Sunday morning, in her 77th year. The deceased was born on Webster Hill, in the town of Western, and was a daughter of Anthony and Martha LeClar. She was married 53 years ago and had lived in Rome 25 years. She was a member of the Wesleyan Methodist Church. Besides her husband, she leaves two sons, Milton G. Butler of Olean, and Solomon Butler of Rome, a daughter Mrs. Robert (Sarah Jane) Barnes of Knoxboro, a brother, Moulton LeClar of Western, and two sisters, Mrs. Sarah Reynolds of Ava and Mrs. Jane Mahedy of Massachusetts.

Roman Citizen July 11, 1895
Ava - Adin Butler, who has been living with his son Solomon, died yesterday at the advanced age of 84 years. The funeral services will be held tomorrow in the Ava M. E. Church. Rev. W. C. Kingsbury will conduct the services. Interment will be made in the Wells Cemetery between North Western and Westernville.
Adin was a carpenter who owned a saw-mill and a stove-mill, turned out 20,000 ash plank oars. He boarded with Pat and Mike Mahedy in 1842/43. (Brother in law)

Children of MARY LECLAR and ADIN BUTLER are:
  i. ALFRED³ BUTLER, b. 15 Nov 1839, Western, Oneida County, NY; d. 06 Oct 1863. He served as a Cpl. in Co. I, 117ᵗʰ Regt. Died of disease at Soldier's Depot, New York. He is buried in the Frenchville Cemetery in Western, Oneida County, NY. The inscription on his tombstone is: Son of A. & M. Butler, age 24 yrs.

.10.   ii.   MILTON G. BUTLER, b. 21 Sep 1841, Western, Oneida County, NY; d. 1912, Ava, Oneida, NY.
11.   iii.   SOLOMON BUTLER, b. 25 Feb 1843, Western, Oneida County, NY; d. 25 May 1918, Vernon, Oneida County, NY.
12.   iv.   SARAH JANE BUTLER, b. 03 Jun 1845, Western, Oneida County, NY; d. 01 Oct 1896, Lee, Oneida County, NY.

4. SARAH[2] LECLAR *(ANTHONY[1])* was born 14 Jul 1822 in Western, Oneida County, NY[15, 16], and died 21 March, 1915 in Western, Oneida Co., NY. She married, 13 April 1846 in Steuben, Oneida Co., NY, CHARLES REYNOLDS, son of DANIEL W. REYNOLDS. He was born 22 May 1822 in Western, Oneida Co., NY, and died 8 February 1892 in Western, Oneida County, NY.[21, 22]. In 1860 they lived in Western. In 1870 and 1892 they lived in Ava, Oneida County, NY.

Both SARAH and CHARLES are buried in the Frenchville Cemetery, Western, Oneida County, NY

By 1880 CHARLES' mother had died and his father, DANIEL, was living with CHARLES and SARAH. Also living with them in 1880 was a grandson, CHARLES M. "Charlie" OPPER, the only son of their daughter, MARTHA ANN (REYNOLDS) OPPER who had died in 1873 shortly after CHARLIE was born. They raised CHARLIE until he married in 1902.

Mrs. Sarah Reynolds
Ava, March 22, 1915. . . This community is again called upon to mourn the death of one who was well known and esteemed, in the person of Mrs. Sarah Reynolds, who passes away on Sunday, March 21, 1915, at noon, at her home, one mile east of this village. Had she lived until July she would have been 93 years of age. She had been ill since last October. Although everything that loving hands could do for her was done the death messenger came to relieve her sufferings.
Mrs. Sarah Reynolds was born on July 14, 1822, in the town of Western and was the daughter of the late Anthony LeClar and Martha Haynes. She was the last of a family of nine children.

8

She was united in marriage on April 13, 1846, to Charles Reynolds in Steuben, by Rev. Waters. After marriage they settled in the town of Western. On November 6, 1875, they moved to their present home oin the town of Ava, where they since resided. Mr. Reynolds died on February 8, 1892.

There were four children born to them. One daughter, Martha, died at the age of 24 years, and a daughter, Mary, died at the age of 4 years and 8 months. There survives one son, Moulton, and one daughter, Jane Reynolds, with whom she made her home.

"Grandma" Reynolds, as she was familiarly known, was very active up till the time of her last illness. She had a remarkable memory for a person of her age and it was very pleasing to converse with her about the early times.

She was a faithful member of the M. E. Church for more than 70 years and attended regularly up to her last sickness. She was a woman of kindly nature and genial disposition and her death will be deeply mourned by family and friends.

Burial will be made beside her husband in Wells Creek Cemetery, in Western.

Children of SARAH LECLAR and CHARLES REYNOLDS are:

    i.   JANE[3] REYNOLDS, b. 09 May 1847, Western, Oneida County, New York[15]; d. 20 May 1935 Western, Oneida Co., NY. Never married, lived with her brother MOULTON. JANE is buried in the Ava Cemetery, Ava, Oneida County, NY.

AVA, May 21, 1935
Jane Reynolds, 88, dies at Oper home.

Miss Jane Reynolds, 88, one of the best known and oldest residents of this section passed away suddenly on Sunday evening at 11:30 at the home of her nephew, Charles Oper, one mile east of this village. Miss Reynolds had been in failing health for several weeks but had been up and about the home most of the time. Jane Reynolds was a daughter of the late Charles and Sarah LeClar Reynolds and was born in the town of Western, May 9, 1847. Her younger life was spent in Western and for a time she lived in Rome; 57 years ago she came to Ava with her parents who settled one mile east of Ava where her father conducted a saw mill and farm.

She had lived in the same home until the death of her brother, Moulton J. Reynolds which occurred Feb. 10. After his death she went to make her home with her nephew, Charles Oper. Miss Reynolds was a member of the Ava M. E. Church.

Surviving is one nephew, Charles M. Oper, Ava; a grand niece, Mrs. Hollis Hurlbut, Ava; three grand nephews, Donald K. Oper, Rome, Norman and Norwood Oper, Ava; a great grand nephew, Jack Oper, Rome; a great grandniece, Martha Beatrice Hurlbut, Ava.

Internment at Ava Cemetery.

13.   ii.   MARTHA ANN REYNOLDS, b. 1849, Western, Oneida County, New York; d. 1873, Western, Oneida County, New York.

iii.   MARY ROSABEL REYNOLDS[16,17], b. 14 Mar 1861, Western, Oneida County, New York[17]; d. 29 Nov 1865, Western, Oneida County, New York[17].

iv.   MOULTON REYNOLDS, b. 12 Jul 1858, Western, Oneida County, New York[18]; d. 10 January 1935. Ava. Oneida Co., NY.. Never married, lived with his sister JANE in Ava. MOULTON is buried in the Ava Cemetery, Ava, Oneida County, NY.

Utica Daily Press,
January 12, 1935 (Tuesday)

Ava - The sudden death of Moulton J. Reynolds occurred at his home Sunday afternoon. Mr. Reynolds was a son of the late Charles and Sarah LeCler Reynolds and was born in Floyd July 21, 1858. The family moved from Floyd to Rome where they lived for some time and 50 years ago came to Ava. They purchased the saw mill, known as the Harger mill, about one mile east of Ava village.

Moulton, with his father, conducted the mill until his father's death and then continued the business himself. Later for many years, Mr. Reynolds nephew, Charles Oper, became associated with him.

Mr. Reynolds never married, he and his sister, Miss Jane Reynolds, have always continued to live together in the family home.

He attended Ava Methodist Episcopal Church. In politics he was a staunch Republican and took a deep and active interest in political affairs and was long one of the Republican leaders in Ava. For many years he served as town committeeman.

Surviving besides his aged sister, Miss Jane Reynolds, is a nephew, Charles Oper, Ava, a grandniece and three grandnephews, and a great-grandniece and nephew. Funeral services will be held Wednesday from his late home.

5. JANE² LECLAR *(ANTHONY¹)* was born 14 Jul 1822 in Western, Oneida County, NY, and died 31 Oct 1894 in Leominster, Worcester, MA.. She married PATRICK MAHEDY 1843 in Rome, Oneida Co., NY. He was born 1813 in Longford County, Ireland, and died 02 Nov 1875 in Shefford, PQ, Canada.

Shortly after the birth of their first child, Sarah Jane, the family moved to Hemingsford, Quebec, Canada, and later moved to Shefford, Quebec, Canada.

After the death of her husband, JANE moved to Massachusetts along with some of her children.

Children of JANE LECLAR and PATRICK MAHEDY are:

14.   i. SARAH JANE8 MAHEDY, b. 1843, Western, Oneida County, New York.
      ii. PETER JOHN MAHEDY, b. 1844, Hemingsford, PQ, Canada.
      iii. ELLEN A. MAHEDY, b. 1844, Hemingsford, PQ, Canada; m. MICHAEL HARPER, 10 Jan 1871, Shefford, PQ, Canada; b. Abt. 1840.
15.   iv. ELIZABETH JANE MAHEDY, b. 1848, Hemingsford, PQ, Canada.
      v. JOHN BAPTISTE MAHEDY, b. Abt. 1850, Hemingsford, PQ, Canada; d. 13 Jul 1911, Shefford, PQ, Canada.
16.   vi. MARTHA MAHEDY, b. Mar 1854, Shefford, PQ, Canada; d. 30 Nov 1944, Quincy, Massachusetts.

vii. MARIE EMACULA MAHEDY, b. 1856, Shefford, PQ, Canada; m. JAMES MCDONALD, Jun 1879, Littleton, NH.

viii. STEPHEN PHILIP MAHEDY, b. 26 Dec 1858, Shefford, PQ, Canada. STEPHEN lived Bet. 1900 - 1930, Leominster, Worcester   Co., Massachusetts (never married)

17.   ix. JAMES ALFRED MAHEDY, b. 1860, Shefford, PQ, Canada; d. 09 Mar 1945, Lawrence, Massachusetts.

x. CHARLES ANTHONY MAHEDY, b. 1862, Shefford, PQ, Canada. Charles is shown, in the 1888 U. S. Army Register of Enlistments, as enlisting at Albany, NY on February 14, 1888. He was discharged on Sept 10, 1888 (no reason given). In 1900 he was single and living in Leominster, Massachusetts with his niece, Mary "Minnie" (Downs) McNeil and her husband Peter McNeil.

xi. MARY ANN MAHEDY, b. 1865, Shefford, PQ, Canada. MARY ANN lived: Bet. 1900 - 1930, Leominster, Worcester Co., Massachusetts (never married)

18.   xii. MARY JANE MAHEDY, b. 16 Dec 1866, Shefford, PQ, Canada; d. 03 Sep 1948, Leominster, Worcester Co., Massachusetts.

Ferdinand LeClar
(1836 - 1882)

Generation No. 3

6. FERDINAND[3] LECLAR *(JOHN BATTIS[2], ANTHONY[1])* was born 01 Mar 1836 in Western, Oneida County, NY[19], and died 30 Mar 1882 in Western, Oneida County, NY. He married, 31 Dec 1857, MARY C. FOX. She was born Mar 1839 in New York[20], daughter of PETER & LANA FOX, and died 10 Dec 1925 in Oneida County, NY[21].

Both FERDINAND and MARY are buried in the Frenchville Cemetery in Western, Oneida County, NY.

Rome Sentinel: April 4, 1882
North Western, Mar. 31 - A sad accident, whereby Ferdinand LeClair, an esteemed and highly respected citizen of the town of Ava, met his death, happened yesterday afternoon. Mr. LeClair
was a well-to-do farmer, and had on his premises a saw mill in which he did sawing for himself and also for some of his neighbors. Yesterday afternoon he went to his mill to work alone. Not returning at the usual supper hour, his son went to the mill for the purpose of calling him and found him fast in a belt in the lower part of the mill, dead. His body had been drawn in in such a way that the machinery was stopped. His left arm and neck were broken. No inquest was held, the family not thinking it necessary. His funeral will be held today at his later residence. A wife and four children are left.
Deceased was a son of Mrs. Rebecca LeClair, who resides on Park Street, in Rome, a brother of Rev. Peter LeClair of Lorraine, Jefferson County, and a brother-in-law of Rev. Robert Flint of Knoxboro, NY.

Rome Sentinel December 10, 1925
Holland Patent - Mrs. Mary C. LeClar passed away at 12:30 o'clock this afternoon at the home of her daughter, Mrs. Hugh Davis of Holland Patent, aged 86 years and eight months.
She is survived by two daughters, Mrs. Hugh Davis with whom she resided, Mrs. Frank Warcup of Westernville, and one son, Peter LeClar of Holland Patent, also 9 grandchildren and 14 great-grandchildren. Her husband, Ferdinand LeClar, formerly of Ava, died several years ago.

Children of FERDINAND LECLAR and MARY FOX are:

19.   i.   CALIFERNA[4] LECLAR, b. Mar 1860, Oneida County, NY. d. 1947, Holland Patent, Oneida County, NY.

20.   ii.   JOHN LECLAR, b. 10 Jan 1862, Oneida County, NY; d. 04 Jun 1920, Verona Station, Oneida County, NY.

iii.   PETER LECLAR, b. Aug 1864, Oneida County, NY (single); d. 1934. PETER never married and lived in his later years with his sister, CALIFERNA and her husband, HUGH DAVIS. PETER is buried in the Frenchville Cemetery in Western, Oneida County, NY.

Holland Patent – 1935
Peter LeClar, 70, dies following long illness.

June 7 - Peter LeClar, 70 died Wednesday at the home of his sister, Mrs. Hugh Davis, after a period of ill health of about a year.

He was born in the town of Ava in 1864, a son of Ferdinand and Mary LeClar. He resided in that town until about 8 years ago when he came to Holland Patent. He never married and was a farmer by occupation.

Surviving besides Mrs. Davis is another sister, Mrs. Frank Warcup of Westernville and several nieces and nephews. Burial will be in Wells Cemetery, Frenchville.

21.   iv.   GERTRUDE "GERTIE" E. LECLAR, b. 18 Dec 1873, Oneida County, NY; d. 10 Jan. 1941, Rome, Oneida, NY.

Rev. Robert Flint
(1833 – 1910)

7. MARY ANN[3] LECLAR *(JOHN BATTIS[2], ANTHONY[1])* was born 30 Jan 1839 in Western, Oneida County, New York, and died 12 Jan 1913 in Black River, Jefferson County, NY. She married ROBERT FLINT, son of JOHN R. FLINT and LANY YERDON. He was born 05 Sep 1833 in Sprout Brook, Montgomery County, NY, and died 13 Jun 1910 in Black River, Jefferson County, NY. The Rev. ROBERT FLINT was a Methodist Minister in Black River.

MARY ANN and ROBERT are buried in the Brookside Cemetery in Watertown, Jefferson County, NY, along with their three sons, CHARLES, WILLIAM, and ROBERT, all physicians.

Children of MARY LECLAR and ROBERT FLINT are:

22. i.   JOSEPHINE FLINT, b. Aug 1859 in Oneida County, NY.
     ii. DR. CHARLES BROOKS[5] FLINT, b. Feb. 1865; d. 12 Sep 1906 in Watertown, NY. He was a Physician in Watertown, Jefferson County, NY. Never married. He is buried in the Brookside Cemetery in Watertown, NY.
23. iii. DR. WILLIAM JOHN FLINT, b. 1867; d. 03 Mar 1947 in Watertown, NY.
     iv. DR. ROBERT JOSEPH FLINT, b. 1872; d. 08 Aug 1904 in Antwerp Village, Jefferson County, NY. He was a Physician in Antwerp Village, Jefferson County, NY. Never married. He is buried in the Brookside Cemetery in Watertown, NY.

8. ELIZABETH[3] LECLAR *(JOHN BATTIS[2], ANTHONY[1])* was born 07 Jan 1841 in Western, Oneida County, New York, and died 08 Nov 1862 in Ava, Oneida Co., NY[1]. She married, 1861 in Oneida County, NY, G. MILTON FLINT, son of PETER ADAM FLINT and CATHERINE WALRADT. He was born 04 Jun 1843 in Oneida Co., NY[1], and died 09 Apr 1894 in Oneida Co., NY[1].

Both ELIZABETH and G. MILTON FLINT are buried in the Flinttown Cemetery, Ava, Oneida Co., NY.

After ELIZABETH's death, G. MILTON md(2) abt 1868, MARTHA GREMS b. July 1842 and d. 9 Feb 1920. MARTHA is buried in Evergreen Cemetery, Lee, Oneida Co., NY.

Child of ELIZABETH LECLAR and G. MILTON FLINT is:
24.   i.   MORTIMER WALTER[4] FLINT, b. 06 Jun 1862, Ava, Oneida Co., NY; d. 07 Mar 1940, Boonville, Oneida County, NY.

9. PETER B.[3] LECLAR *(JOHN BATTIS[2], ANTHONY[1])* was born 20 Nov 1849 in Western, Oneida County, New York[44], and died 09 Mar 1917 in Jeffersonville, Fayette County, Ohio[45]. He married (1) CARRIE WHITE in 1875. She was born Mar 1857 in New York[46,47], and died Abt. 1903 in Lucas County, Ohio?. He married (2) ESTHER MOSIER Abt. 1905. She was born 24 Mar 1867 in Van Wert County, Ohio[48], and died 18 Sep 1935 in Tiffin, Seneca County, Ohio[48]. PETER was an ordained Methodist Minister.

PETER LECLAR is buried in Fern Cliff Cemetery, Jeffersonville, Fayette Co., Ohio. ESTHER MOSIER is buried in Greenlawn Cemetery, Tiffin, Seneca County, Ohio.

Daily Gazette - March 10, 1917, Xenia, Ohio
... the Rev Peter Leclar, Pastor of the Methodist Churches in Spring Valley died Friday at his home in Jeffersonville of an ?? He had been seriously ill for four... Leclar was one of the oldest Ministers in the Methodist Protestant Church. . .

Daily Gazette - March 14, 1917, Xenia, Ohio
.. the many friends of Rev Peter Leclar were very sorry to learn of his death . . .

Children of PETER LECLAR and CARRIE WHITE are:
        i.   JESSIE BATTES[4] LECLAR, b. 01 Jun 1884, Lorraine, Jefferson County, NY[28]; d. 23 Jun 1950, Tiffin, Seneca County, Ohio. JESSIE was living with ESTHER and CAROLINE MOSIER, her sister in Tiffin, Ohio in 1818 when he registered for the draft in WWI. He is

also shown living with CAROLINE MOSIER when he registered for the draft in 1942 for WWII. JESSIE never married.

ii. JAMES WALKER LECLAR[29], b. 13 Dec 1889, Springfield, Ohio[29]; m. ZELMA J., Bet. 1915 – 1920 in Minnesota; b. c1888, in Minnesota. Prior to moving to Minneapolis, Minn., JAMES is shown, in the 1915 North Dakota census, living with his brother LEO C. LECLAR in Dunn, North Dakota. We have not found the record of his death or burial.

iii. DR. LEO COWLING LECLAR, b. 15 Apr 1891, Springfield, Ohio[29]; d. 04 Mar 1924, Twin Bridges, Montana[30]; m. 14 May 1921 MYRTLE FRANCIS "BABE" EDWARDS, dau. Of REUBEN DAVID EDWARDS and ELIZABETH JANE REDFERN, in Butte, Silver Bow, Montana[31]; b. 25 Apr 1901, Twin Bridges, Madison, Montana; d. 28 Nov 1957, San Bruno, San Mateo County, California.

LEO graduated from Washington Court House High School, Ohio in 1909.

LEO was a Physician/Surgeon having graduated from medical school at the College of Medicine, Ohio State University in 1913. He was licensed to practice in Ohio, North Dakota, and Minnesota. He had practiced medicine at Columbus, Ohio; Halliday, ND; Twin Bridges, MT; and Virginia City, MT. The cause of his early death was epidemic (lethargic) encephalitis.

10. MILTON[3] G. BUTLER (MARY A.[2] LECLAIRE, ANTHONY[1] LECLAR,) born 21 Sep 1841 in Western, Oneida County, NY, and died 1912 in Ava, Oneida County, NY. He married JENNIE M. in 1867. She was born Sep 1843 in New York. MILTON was a carpenter by trade. The family lived in Brockport, Monroe Co.,NY then in Cattaraugus County, NY near Olean.

Children of MILTON & JENNIE BUTLER are:

i. FLERA M. BUTLER, b. 1867, New York
ii. CHILD BUTLER, b. abt. 1873, d. bef. 1880.
iii. TINA BUTLER, b. 1879, New York

Solomon & Esther (Mahedy) Butler

11. SOLOMON BUTLER *(MARY A.³ LECLAIRE, ANTHONY²*
LECLAR, JOHN¹ LECLERC?) was born 25 Feb 1843 in Oneida
Co., NY, and died 25 May 1918 in Vernon, Oneida Co., NY. He
married, in 1883, ESTHER A. MAHEDY, dau of MICHAEL
MAHEDY and ESTHER GILLETT. She was born 10 Feb 1852 in
Sherrington, PQ, Canada and died 06 Apr 1927 in Verona, Oneida
Co., NY.
SOLOMON is buried in the Vernon Village Cemetery, Vernon, NY

Children of SOLOMON & ESTHER MAHEDY BUTLER are:

      i. ZORA WINIFRED BUTLER, b. 21 Jan 1890, New
         York; d. 28 July 1987, Lowville, Lewis County, NY.
         (never married)

25.   ii. JOSEPH MILTON BUTLER, b. 01 June 1891, NY,
         d. 08 Sep 1990, Lowville, Lewis County, NY.

12 SARAH JANE³ BUTLER *(MARY A.² LECLAIRE, ANTHONY¹*
LECLAR) was born 03 Jun 1845 in Western, Oneida County, NY,
and died 01 Oct 1896 in Lee, Oneida Co., NY. She married
ROBERT BARNES, son of RICHARD & CATHARINE HUGHS
BARNES. He was born 01 Jun 1848, in Utica, and died 29 Oct
1925 in Lee, Oneida Co., NY..
    Both SARAH and ROBERT are buried in Evergreen Cemetery,
Lee, Oneida County, NY

Children of SARAH BUTLER and ROBERT BARNES are:

      i. RICHARD⁵ D. BARNES, b. 30 Dec. 1868 in Lee,
         Oneida County; d. 27 Jun 1874 in Lee, Oneida County
         RICHARD is buried in Evergreen Cemetery, Lee,
         Oneida County, NY.

26   ii. MARY C. BARNES, b. Aug 1869, Oneida County; d.
         20 Jan 1956.

    iii. ADIN P. BARNES, b. 26 Dec 1873, Ava, Oneida
         County; d. 24 July 1965 in NY. Lived 1930 in Verona,
         Oneida County (single). ADIN P. BARNES is buried
         in Evergreen Cemetery, Oneida County.

    iv. ALFRED BARNES, b. Abt. 1875.

    v. LILLIE BARNES, b. 09 Apr 1883, Lee, Oneida Co.; d.
        05 July 1895, Lee, Oneida Co, NY. LILLIE is buried in
        Evergreen Cemetery, Lee, Oneida County.

13. MARTHA ANN[3] REYNOLDS *(SARAH[2] LECLAR, ANTHONY[1])* was born 1849 in Western, Oneida County, New York, and died 1873 in Western, Oneida County, New York. She married MARTIN J. OPPER, abt. 1870. He was born Oct 1845 in Germany.

MARTHA is buried in Frenchville Cemetery, Western, Oneida County, NY

MARTIN OPPER remarried, after the death of MARTHA, and had other children.

Child of MARTHA REYNOLDS and MARTIN OPPER is:
27.   i.   CHARLES M. 'CHARLIE'[5] OPPER, b. Dec 1871, Western, Oneida County, New York.

14. SARAH JANE[3] MAHEDY *(JANE[2] LECLAR, ANTHONY[1]* LeClar)* was born 1843 in Western, Oneida County, New York. She married, 01 Jul 1867 in Shefford, PQ, Canada, WILLIAM COBURN, son of MICHAEL COBURN and ELIZABETH RAY. He was born 1840 in Canada.

Children of SARAH MAHEDY and WILLIAM COBURN are:
        i.   EMILY J.[4] COBURN, b. 1871, Shefford, PQ, Canada.
       ii.   FLORA M. COBURN, b. 1873, Shefford, PQ, Canada.
      iii.   SARAH G. COBURN, b. 1877, Shefford, PQ, Canada.
       iv.   ALFRED COBURN, b. 1880, Shefford, PQ, Canada.
        v.   ALBERT COBURN, b. 1880, Shefford, PQ, Canada.

15. ELIZABETH JANE³ MAHEDY *(JANE² LECLAR, ANTHONY¹)* was born 1848 in Hemingsford, PQ, Canada. She married, 17 Jul 1876 in Shefford, PQ, Canada, HENRY MCCAFFREY. He was born 1843 in Shefford, PQ, Canada, and died 05 May 1911 in Montreal, Canada.

Children of ELIZABETH MAHEDY and HENRY MCCAFFREY are:

    i. MARGARITE⁴ MCCAFFREY, b. Apr 1878, Shefford, PQ, Canada.

    ii. ELIZABETH MCCAFFREY, b. Abt. 1880, Savage's Mills, PQ, Canada.

    iii. CHARLES MCCAFFREY, b. Abt. 1882, Savage's Mills, PQ, Canada.

16. MARTHA³ MAHEDY *(JANE² LECLAR, ANTHONY¹)* was born Mar 1854 in Shefford, PQ, Canada, and died 30 Nov 1944 in Quincy, Massachusetts. She married (1) 20 Oct 1873 in Shefford, PQ, Canada, JOHN MCNEIL. He was born Abt. 1850 in Shefford, PQ, Canada, and died 1879 in Shefford, PQ, Canada. She married (2) 1879 in Shefford, PQ, Canada, RICHARD GALLAGHER. He was born Sep 1850 in County Longford, Ireland, and died 02 Oct 1902 in Barre, Washington Co., VT. MARTHA immigrated to the U.S. In 1878.

Children of MARTHA MAHEDY and JOHN MCNEIL are:

    i. JOHN³ MCNEIL, b. 1875, Shefford, PQ, Canada.

    ii. PETER MCNEIL, b. Jan 1875, Shefford, PQ, Canada; m. MARY "MINNIE" DOWNS, 1899, Massachusetts; b. Dec 1875, New York.

Children of MARTHA MAHEDY & RICHARD GALLAGHER are:

28.   iii. CHARLES RICHARD⁴ GALLAGHER, b. 01 Apr 1882, Roxbury, VT.

    iv. JAMES P. GALLAGHER, b. 17 Mar 1884, Barre, Washington Co., VT.

29.   v. MARY "MAMIE" GALLAGHER, b. Jan 1887, Barre, Washington Co., VT; d. Quincy, Massachusetts.

      vi. JOHN STEPHEN GALLAGHER[86], b. 09 Sep 1889, Barre, Washington Co., VT[86]; d. 08 Jan 1937, Barre, Washington Co., VT (never married). JOHN was a blacksmith in Barre.

30.   vii. LUKE FRANCIS GALLAGHER, b. 01 Jan 1892, Barre, Washington Co., VT.

      viii. WILLIAM ANTHONY GALLAGHER[88], b. 31 Mar 1894, Barre, Washington Co., VT[88]; d. 05 Jul 1949, of Tuberculosis in Waterbury, Washington Co., VT (never married).

17. JAMES ALFRED[3] MAHEDY *(JANE[2] LECLAR, ANTHONY[1])* was born 1860 in Shefford, PQ, Canada, and died 09 Mar 1945 in Lawrence, Massachusetts. He married, in 1886 in Shefford, PQ, Canada, ANNIE LAWLOR. She was born in 1862. JAMES emigrated in 1915 from Canada to the U.S./Massachusetts. In the U.S. Census records, James was listed by his middle name, Alfred. In 1920 he was living in Leominster, Mass with his daughter Mary, her husband Leo Guilfoyle and his single daughter, Cora. In 1930 he was living in Kingston, Rockingham, NH with Mary & Leo and their family, along with Cora and her husband Frank Guilfoyle..

Children of JAMES MAHEDY and ANNIE LAWLOR are:

      i. EDWARD[4] MAHEDY, b. 1887, Shefford, PQ, Canada; d. 1888, Shefford, PQ, Canada.

      ii. JAMES MAHEDY, b. 1889, Shefford, PQ, Canada; d. 1890, Shefford, PQ, Canada.

      iii. ERNEST MAHEDY, b. 1891, Shefford, PQ, Canada; d. 1892, Shefford, PQ, Canada.

      iv. ARTHUR MAHEDY, b. 1893, Shefford, PQ, Canada; d. 1925, Western Canada.

31.   v. MARY E. MAHEDY, b. 09 Jun 1895, Shefford, PQ, Canada.

      vi. CORA A. MAHEDY, b. 1897, Shefford, PQ, Canada; d. Lawrence, Massachusetts; md. in 1923 in Massachusetts[89] , FRANK B. GUILFOYLE; b. 04 Apr 1891, Lawrence, Massachusetts.

18. MARY JANE "JENNIE"[3] MAHEDY *(JANE[2] LECLAR, ANTHONY[1])* was born 16 Dec 1866 in Shefford, PQ, Canada, and died 03 Sep 1948 in Leominster, Worcester Co., Massachusetts. She married, in 1888, JOSEPH DOWNS. He was born May 1866 in New York[90], and died 01 Jun 1929 in Leominster, Worcester Co., Massachusetts.

Children of MARY MAHEDY and JOSEPH DOWNS are:

	i.	MARGARET MARY BRIDGET[4] DOWNS, b. 12 Aug 1889, Mineville, NY; d. Baltimore, MD.
	ii.	MARY ELLEN "NELLIE" DOWNS, b. 18 Sep 1890; d. North Carolina.
	iii.	WALTER EDWARD DOWNS, b. 03 Sep 1893, Leominster, Worcester Co., Massachusetts; d. 1979.
	iv.	MARY MARTHA DOWNS, b. Sep. 1895, Leominster, Worcester Co., Massachusetts; d. Leominster, Worcester Co., Massachusetts (died young).
32.	v.	CLAYTON J. DOWNS, b. 31 Mar 1899, Leominster, Worcester Co., Massachusetts; d. 1946.
	vi.	MARTHA DOWNS, b. 1903, Leominster, Worcester Co., Massachusetts; d. 1905, Leominster, Worcester Co., Massachusetts.
	vii.	PHILIP A. DOWNS, b. 19 Jan 1907, Leominster, Worcester Co., Massachusetts; d. Panama Canal Zone.
33.	viii.	MARY MADELINE DOWNS, b. 24 May 1912, Leominster, Worcester Co., Massachusetts; d. Leominster, Worcester Co., Massachusetts.

Hugh Davis & Califerna LeClar Family

L-to-R: Lloyd, Hugh, Leroy, Lula, Harold, Califerna

28

Generation No. 4

19. CALIFERNA[4] LECLAR *(FERDINAND[3], JOHN BATTIS[2], ANTHONY[1])[91]* was born 22 Apr 1860 in Oneida County, NY[92], and died 1947 in Holland Patent, Oneida County, NY. She married, 26 Nov 1885 in Ava, Oneida County, NY[93] HUGH R. DAVIS, son of EDWARD & CATHERINE DAVIS. He was born Jun 1859 in New York[94], and died Aft. 1947 in Oneida Co., NY.

HOLLAND PATENT
COUPLE OBSERVES 58TH ANNIVERSARY
  Holland Patent, Nov 26 (1943) --- Mr. and Mrs. Hugh R. Davis are today marking their 58th wedding anniversary at their home here. No celebration is planned as Mrs. Davis has been ill the past week.
  They were married in the Methodist parsonage in Lee Center with the Rev. John Simpson officiating. Mrs. Davis was formerly of Ava and Mr. Davis of West Branch, where he operated a Rome-Constableville stage and mail route. Later he was named postmaster and also operated a store.
  They came to Holland Patent in 1900 and operated the John Edwards farm for 12 years, then they bought the Fred H. Peabody farm, a half mile from this village on the Holland Patent - Stittville Road.
  Both are members of the Holland Patent Presbyterian Church. Mr. Davis has served as elder for the past 37 years. Mrs. Davis is a member of church organizations and Holland Patent-Stittville WCTU.
  They have four children: Leroy F. Davis, Floyd; Harold E. Davis, Stittville; Lloyd H. Davis, Rome; and Mrs David E. Jones, Holland Patent, and several grandchildren. They had two grandsons in the Army but one in the Army Air Corps was lost at sea.

Mrs. Hugh Davis dies at Age 86
Native of Ava was ill past year

Holland Patent -- Mrs. Califerna L. Davis, 86, wife of Hugh Davis, died Sunday at the home of her daughter, Mrs. David E. Jones, after an illness of a year.

She was born in Ava, April 22, 1860, a daughter of Ferdinand and Mary Fox LeClar. On Nov. 26, 1885 in Ava she was married to Mr. Davis and the couple marked their 61st anniversary last Thanksgiving.

Mrs. Davis and her husband came to Holland Patent in 1900 and have since lived here. She was a member of the Presbyterian Church and its societies and a member of the Holland Patent-Stittville WCTU.

Surviving are her husband; the daughter at whose home she died; three sons, LeRoy and Harold, Stittville, and Lloyd, Rome; also ten grandchildren and six great grandchildren.

Funeral services will be held at the home of Mrs. Jones on Wednesday at the convenience of the family and interment will be made in Townsend Cemetery, Stittville.

Children of CALIFERNA LECLAR and HUGH DAVIS are:

34.	i.	LEROY F.[5] DAVIS, b. 18 Jul 1890, New York; d. Dec 1973, Ithaca, Tompkins Co., NY.
35.	ii.	HAROLD E. DAVIS, b. 16 Aug 1892, West Branch, New York; d. 29 Apr 1979, Stittville, Oneida County, NY.
	iii.	LLOYD H. DAVIS, b. Apr 1894, New York[97]; md. FLORENCE PARSONS FARMER; b. Abt. 1895. LLOYD was a National Grange Insurance Agent
36.	iv.	LULA M. DAVIS, b. Jul 1897, New York; d. 1988.

John & Nellie R. (Hogan) LeClar

14. JOHN[5] LECLAR *(FERDINAND[4], JOHN BATTIS[3], ANTHONY[2], JOHN[1] LECLERC?)* was born 10 Jan 1862 in Oneida County, NY[34], and died 04 Jun 1920 in Verona Station, Oneida County, NY[34]. He married NELLIE R. HOGAN in 1886, daughter of MICHAEL and SARA J. HOGAN . She was born 05 Nov 1863 in Western, Oneida County, New York, and died 14 Jun 1945 in Chenango Memorial Hospital, Norwich, Chenango County, NY. NELLIE was a member of the First Methodist Church, Rome, NY.

At the time of her death, NELLIE was living with her daughter NELLIE GOODRICH and her husband JAMES V. GOODRICH in Norwich, Chenango County, NY.

Both JOHN LECLAR and NELLIE (HOGAN) LECLAR are buried in the Westernville Cemetery, Westernville, Oneida County, NY

Utica Daily Press June 5, 1920
Rome June 4 - John LeClar died at 5 pm today at his home at Verona Station. He had been out of health for three years. He was born in the town of Western January 10, 1862, son of Ferdinand LeClar. He is survived by his wife, who was formerly Nellie R. Hogan, and two children, Jesse N. and Nellie V. of Western, and his mother, Mrs. Mary LeClar of Holland Patent, and a brother, Peter, of Holland Patent, and two sisters, Mrs. Hugh Davis of Holland Patent, Mrs. Frank Warcup of Westernville and five grandchildren. The funeral will be held at the house Tuesday and at the M. E. Church in Westernville.

OBITUARY - NORWICH, 1945
PRAYER SERVICE TONIGHT
A prayer service will be held at the Breese Funeral Home at 8 o'clock Friday night for Mrs. Nellie H. LeClar, whose death occurred at Chenango Memorial Hospital Thursday noon.

Funeral services are to be held Sunday afternoon at 2 o'clock at the Griffin & Aldridge Funeral Home in Rome. Burial is to be made at Westernville.

The deceased had been ill but two weeks prior to her death. She was born Nov. 5, 1863 at Hillside, N.Y., town of Western, a daughter of the late Michael and Sarah J. Hogan. She was united in marriage with John LeClar of Ava, N.Y., Dec 23, 1885 by the Rev. Simpson of Lee Center. Mr. LeClar died June 4, 1920. Four children were born of the union.

Most of her long life was spent in and around Rome. For several years she had been a frequent visitor in the home of her daughter, Mrs. James Goodrich of East Norwich. A year and a half ago she disposed of her home in Rome and came to make her home with her daughter and family.

She was possessed of a very pleasing personality and was beloved by all who knew her. She was affectionately known as "Grandma" by her many friends. Mrs. LeClar was very spry and active for one of her years. Only recently, on Mother's day, she received a beautiful potted plant for being the eldest mother present at the Broad Street Methodist Church.

She was a life-long Methodist. For many years was a member of the Firsts M. E. Church at Rome and only last Easter had her letter transferred to Broad Street church at Norwich.

There survive two children, Jesse LeClar of North Western and Mrs. James V. Goodrich of East Norwich; one sister, Mrs. Sarah C. Cummings of Rome; six grandchildren, Clayton Cummings of North Western, Corp. James Cummings of Fort Jackson, S. C. , Harold LeClar and Mrs. Albert Nestle of North Western, and Joyce and Edna Goodrich of Norwich; also two great-grandchildren, Richard LaClar and Rodney Nestle of North Western. There are also several nieces and nephews.

Rome Sentinel June 15, 1945

Mrs. Nellie H. LeClar died at the Chenango Memorial Hospital, Norwich, yesterday following an illness of a few weeks.

The daughter of the late Michael and Sara J. Hogan, Mrs. LeClar was born Nov. 5, 1863, in Hillside, Town of Western. She was married to John LeClar in 1885. He died June 4, 1920. She spent her entire life in the Town of Western with the exception of the last 18 months which she spent with her daughter, Mrs. James Goodrich, East Norwich.

Mrs. LeClar was a member of the First Methodist Church, Rome, and later was a member of the Norwich Methodist Church.

Besides her daughter, she is survived by a son, Jesse LeClar, North Western, a sister, Mrs. Sara Cummings, Rome, six grandchildren, two great-grandchildren, and several nieces and nephews.

Funeral services will be held from the Griffin & Aldridge Funeral Home Sunday. Interment will be in Westernville Cemetery.

Children of JOHN LECLAR and NELLIE HOGAN are:

37.　　　i.　JESSE FERDINAND[5] LECLAR, b. 17 Aug 1887, Oneida County, NY; d. 14 Apr 1975, North Western, Oneida County, NY.

38.   ii. FLORENCE E. LECLAR, b. 02 Oct 1888, Oneida
            County, NY; d. 03 Jul 1917, Western, Oneida County,
            New York.
       iii. MABEL G. LECLAR[99], b. 25 Dec 1894, Oneida
            County, NY; d. 10 Jan 1896, Western, Oneida County,
            New York[100].
39.   iv. NELLIE HOGAN LECLAR, b. 21 Oct 1897, Western,
            Oneida County, NY; d. 17 Apr 1988, Norwich,
            Chenango County, New York.

Florence E., Mabel G. , and Jesse Ferdinand LeClar

(About 1897)

Frank & Gertrude (LeClar) Warcup
and children (top-to-bottom)
Florence, John, Harold

21. GERTRUDE "GERTIE" E.[4] LECLAR (*FERDINAND*[3], *JOHN BATTIS*[2], *ANTHONY*[1]) was born 18 Dec 1873 in East Ava, Oneida County, NY[101], and died 10 Jan 1941 in Rome, Oneida, NY[101,102]. She married FRANK E. WARCUP 03 Dec 1901 in North Western, Oneida County, NY[103], son of JOHN WARCUP and CYNTHIA O. HARRINGTON. He was born 28 Oct 1872 in Western, Oneida County, New York[104], and died 27 Oct 1949 in Westernville, Oneida County, NY[105,106]. FRANK was a carpenter in Rome, NY.

Both GERTRUDE and FRANK are buried in the Frenchville Cemetery in Western, Oneida County, New York, as are all three of their children.

OBITUARY - Rome Sentinel, January 10, 1941

Westernville - The death of Mrs. Frank Warcup occurred at 1:20 am Friday at her home, 327 Kossuth Street, Rome. Gertie Leclar was born in East Ava on December 18, 1873, daughter of the late Ferdinand and Mary Fox LeClar. She was married to Frank Warcup in North Western on December 3, 1901, and resided in their newly built home in Westernville. In 1925 they built a home at 327 Kossuth Street, Rome and have resided there since. She had been in ill health for the last five years and had been confined to her bed for the past three weeks. She was a member of the Ladies Aid Society of the Westernville Methodist Church and was active in church work as long as her health permitted. Surviving besides her husband are a daughter, Mrs. George Reese, Westernville, two sons, John at home, and Harold of Rome, one sister, Mrs. Hugh davis of Holland Patent, two grandchildren, Howard and Linda Warcup, and several nieces and nephews. Funeral services will be held at the home of her daughter, Mrs. George Reese, Westernville on Sunday. Interment will be in Westernville Cemetery.

OBITUARY - FRANK WARCUP

Frank Warcup, 76, Westernville, retired carpenter and cabinetmaker, died October 27, 1949, in the home of his daughter, Mrs. George Reese, Westernville. He had been in failing health for the past 4 years, and seriously ill for 4 months.

Born in the Town of Western, October 28, 1872, he was the son of John and Cynthia Harrington Warcup. On December 3, 1901 in North Western he married the former Gertie LeClar, who died January 10, 1941. He lived all his life in Westernville except for a few years before his wife's death when they resided at 327 Kossuth Street, Rome.

He was known for his skill in the construction of frame barns. He erected his first building when he was 13, and at 14 constructed a school on the River Road, 1/2 mile south of North Western. It is now in use as a residence.

He attended the Westernville Methodist Church and for several years was a trustee.

Surviving in addition to his daughter are two sons, John F. and Harold O. Warcup of Rome; three brothers, Stanley and William of Westernville and Robert, Oneida; and 4 grandchildren.

. . . Interment will be in Westernville Cemetery.

Children of GERTRUDE LECLAR and FRANK WARCUP are:

      i.   FLORENCE[5] WARCUP, b. 02 May 1905, Western, Oneida County, New York[108]; d. 16 Oct 1999, Westernville, Oneida County, NY[108]; m. (1) GEORGE REESE; m. (2) ARTHUR B. WALSWORTH[109], 30 Apr 1966, by Rev. Chester Lippy, in the Westernville, Presbyterian Church, Oneida Co., NY.[109]

          FLORENCE was a teacher in ROME, NY.

          FLORENCE WARCUP REESE is buried in the Westernville Cemetery in Westernville, Oneida Co., NY.

          Boonville Herald, Boonville, NY May 25, 1994, Page 5 HISTORICAL SOCIETY -- The Town of Western Historical Society held the annual dinner meeting at Woods Valley Ski Chalet on Thursday, May 12. Past historians **Florence Walsworth** *and* **Marion DiCarlo** *were honored, both receiving the Golden Quill Award. . . .*

40.   ii. *JOHN F WARCUP, b. 10 Dec 1907, Westernville, Oneida County, New York; d. 24 Dec 1975, Rome Hospital, Rome, Oneida County, New York.*

41.   iii. *HAROLD OLIN WARCUP, b. 20 Jun 1909, Western, Oneida County, New York; d. 01 Jan 1983, Western, Oneida County, New York.*

22. JOSEPHINE[4] FLINT *(MARY ANN[3] LECLAR, JOHN BATTIS[2], ANTHONY[1])* was born Aug 1859 in Oneida County, NY[113,114,115]. She married ROMAINE DELMONT GIBBS[116] 1891[117], son of JAMES GIBBS and MARYETTE E. KENNEDY. He was born Mar 1848 in Jefferson County, NY[117].

Children of JOSEPHINE FLINT and ROMAINE GIBBS are:
42.   i.   CHARLES BROOKS. F.[5] GIBBS, b. 27 Sep 1894,
             Jefferson County, NY; d. 02 Aug 2000, Rochester,
             Monroe Co. NY.
43.   ii. DR. ROBERT FLINT D. GIBBS, b. 05 Mar 1898,
             Jefferson County, NY; d. Mar 1975, Seneca Falls, NY.

23. Dr. WILLIAM JOHN FLINT *(MARY ANN[4] LECLAR, JOHN
BATTIS[3], ANTHONY[2], JOHN[1] LECLERC?)* was born 1867 in
Oneida County, NY and died 03 March 1947 in Watertown,
Jefferson County, NY. He married, 15 June 1892, ANNA GOOD-
FELLOW, b. 13 Dec 1870 in New York.
     WILLIAM JOHN FLINT is buried in Brookside Cemetery,
Watertown, Jefferson Co., NY.

Child of WILLIAM & ANNA GOODFELLOW FLINT is:
     i.   MILDRED IRENE FLINT, b. 10 Nov 1893, Watertown,
          Jefferson County, NY.

24. MORTIMER WALTER[4] FLINT *(ELIZABETH[3] LECLAR, JOHN
BATTIS[2], ANTHONY[1])* was born 06 Jun 1862 in Ava, Oneida Co.,
NY[124,125], and died 07 Mar 1940 in Boonville, Oneida County, NY[126].
He married ELLA WILLIAMS[127] 25 Apr 1882 in Boonville, Oneida
County, NY[127]. She was born Feb 1864[128], and died Aug 1936 in
Oneida Co., NY[129]. They were members of the Ava Methodist
Church. MORTIMER was a farmer.
     Both MORTIMER and ELLA are buried in the Ava Cemetery,
Ava, Oneida Co., NY.

Boonville, March 8, 1940
     *Mortimer W. Flint, 77, retired farmer and former resident of Ava and
West Leyden, died Thursday night at the home of his son Walter Flint,
Schuyler Street, after an illness of eight months.*
     *He was born in Ava, June 6, 1862, a son of the late Milton and
Elizabeth LeClair Flint. On April 25, 1882, at Boonville, he married
Miss Ella Williams, the Rev. Guile performing the ceremony. Mrs. Flint
died in August, 1936.*

Mr. Flint was a farmer in Ava for 43 years and then lived in West Leyden for several years, coming to the home of his son four years ago. He was a member of Ava Methodist Church which he served for a time as trustee. He was a member of Baron Steuben Lodge, 264, F. & A. M., Lee Center. He was a Democrat in politics and served the Town of Ava as collector for two terms, and also served as a justice of the peace and as Welfare officer.

Surviving besides his son at whose home he died, is a brother, Grover C. Flint, Lee Center. A daughter, Ida Flint Meyers died 27 years ago.

Funeral services will be held at the Flint home on Schuyler St., on Sunday at 2 pm, the Rev. James Benes, pastor of the West Leyden and Ava Churches, officiating. Burial will be in Ava Cemetery.

Children of MORTIMER FLINT and ELLA WILLIAMS are:

    i.   WALTER[5] FLINT, b. 28 Jun 1902, Oneida County, NY[130]; d. 04 Apr 1986, Boonville, Oneida County, NY[130]; m. THELMA TAFT.[131]; b. 1903[131]; d. 05 Aug 1989[131].

   ii.   IDA FLINT, b. Oct 1893, Oneida County, NY; d. 1913, Oneida County, NY; m. _____ MEYERS; b. Abt. 1890.

Joseph Milton Butler and his sister Zora Winifred Butler

Zora Winifred Butler and Bernice (Senecal) Butler

Joseph Milton Butler

25. JOSEPH MILTON BUTLER *(SOLOMON[4] MARY A.[3] LECLAIRE, ANTHONY[2] LECLAR, JOHN[1] LECLERC?)*was born 01 June 1891 in New York, and died 08 Sept 1990 in Lowville, Lewis County, NY. He married, 10 Apr 1926, BERNICE E. SENECAL in Oriskany Falls, NY, daughter of CHARLES LEON SENECAL and IDA MARCHAND. She was born 29 July 1896 in Cleveland, NY, and died 27 July 1988 in Lowville, Lewis County, NY.

JOSEPH and BERNICE are buried in St. Patrick's Cemetery, Oneida, NY.

Butlers To Note 50th

LOWVILLE - *Mr. and Mrs. Joseph Butler, 7675 Park Ave, Lowville, formerly of Utica, will celebrate their 50th wedding anniversary today at an open house at the Lowville Grange Hall, Lowville.*

Butler and the former Bernice Senecal were married April 10, 1926, in Oriskany Falls.

The couple has two daughters, Mrs. Frederick Martin, Lowville, and Mrs. Edward Gassner, Wellsboro, PA, nine grandchildren; and a great-granddaughter.

OBITUARY

Bernice S. Butler, age 92, of Valley View Apts., Lowville, died Wednesday, July 27, 1988 at the Lewis County General Hospital where she had been a patient for a day.

A Mass of the Resurrection will be at 10 a.m. Saturday in St. Peter's Church with Rev. Bernard Christman, Pastor, officiating. Burial will be held at 2 that afternoon in St. Patrick's Cemetery, Oneida. Calling hours will be 2-4 and 7-9, Friday, at the Donald F.Virkler Funeral Home, where the Rosary will be recited at 8:30 Friday evening. Contributions may be made to either the Faxton Foundation, 1676 Sunset Av., Utica, NY 13502 or St. Peter's Church Memorial Fund.

Surviving are her husband, Joseph, two daughters. Mrs. Frederick (Barbara) Martin, RD, Lowville, and Mrs Edward (Shirley) Gassner, New Hartford; nine grandchildren; 11 great-grandchildren; two sisters-in-law, Mrs Doris Senecal Flynn, FL. and Mrs Agnes Senecal Manseau, Baldwinsville; and two nieces, Mrs John (Gail) Carriere, MD., and Mrs. Donald (Rosemary) Jones, Oriskany Falls.

Born in Cleveland, NY on July 29, 1896, a daughter of Charles and Ida Marchand Senecal, she moved to Oriskany Falls in 1911, where she graduated from high school in 1915. She was later graduated from the Faxton School of Nursing, Utica, in 1918. She married Joseph M. Butler, April 10, 1926, at St. Joseph's Church, Oriskany Falls, with Rev. Calvin Gordon officiating. She worked as a nurse at Faxton Hospital, Utica, Lewis County General Hospital, Lowville, and Oneida General Hospital, Oneida, and retired in 1970. Burial will be in St. Patrick's Cemetery, Oneida, NY.

Children of JOSEPH BUTLER and BERNICE SENECAL are:

    i.   BARBARA[5] BUTLER, b. 1927, New York; m. FREDERICK MARTIN; b. Abt. 1925. Lived in Lowville, Lewis County, NY

   ii.   SHIRLEY BUTLER, b. 1928, New York; m. EDWARD GASSNER; b. Abt. 1928. Lived in New Hartford, Oneida County, NY

26. MARY C.[4] BARNES *(SARAH JANE[3] BUTLER, MARY ANN[2] LECLAR, ANTHONY[1])[134]* was born Aug 1869 in Oneida County, NY, and died 20 Jan 1956. She married JOHN RUHM abt. 1891 in Oneida County. He was born Apr 1868 in New York, and died 23 Aug 1950.

Both MARY and JOHN RUHM are buried in Evergreen Cemetery, Lee, Oneida County, NY.

Children of MARY BARNES and JOHN RUHM are:

44.   i.   RAYMOND ROBERT RUHM, b. 14 Apr 1893, Munnsville, Madison County, NY; died 13 Jun 1954.

       ii.   FLORA B. RUHM, b. Nov 1894, New York; d. Oct 1974, Utica, Oneida County, NY.

45.   iii.   FRANCES M. RUHM, b. 27 June 1896, New York; d. Feb 1983 in Houston, Texas.

      iv.   MYRTLE LORETA J. RUHM, b. May 1898, New York.

       v.   KENNETH RUHM, b. 1906, New York. In 1930 KENNETH was single, living with his parents.

(Right-to-Left)
Charles M. "Charlie" Opper
Charlie's oldest son: Donald K. Opper
Charlie's maternal grandmother: Sarah (LeClar) Reynolds
Charlie's aunt (his mother's sister): Jane Reynolds

46

27. CHARLES M. 'CHARLIE'[14] OPPER *(MARTHA ANN[3] REYNOLDS, SARAH[2] LECLAR, ANTHONY[1])*[139] was born Dec 1871 in Western, Oneida County, New York[140]. He married BEATRICE L. "BEE" KILTS[141] in 1902[141], daughter of MATTHEW & JULIA J. KILTS. She was born Feb 1876 in New York.

Children of CHARLES OPPER and BEATRICE KILTS are:
-     i. DONALD K.[5] OPER, b. 12 Sep 1902, Ava, Oneida, NY; d. 16 Jul 1990.
- 46.   ii. DOROTHY G. OPPER, b. 1905, Ava, Oneida, NY; d. 27 Mar 1962, Rome, Oneida, NY.
-   iii. NORMAN W. OPPER, b. 21 Mar 1918, Ava, Oneida, NY; d. 31 Mar 2001, Boonville, Oneida County, NY.
-   iv. NORWOOD C. OPPER, b. 1918, Ava, Oneida, NY.

28. CHARLES RICHARD[4] GALLAGHER *(MARTHA[3] MAHEDY, JANE[2] LECLAR, ANTHONY[1])*[142] was born 01 Apr 1882 in Roxbury, VT[142]. He married, 01 Jul 1907 in Montpelior, VT, HARRIET E. WHITE. She was born Abt. 1887. CHARLES was a blacksmith.

Children of CHARLES GALLAGHER and HARRIET WHITE are:
- 47.   i. LEO R.[5] GALLAGHER, b. 09 Aug 1908, Barre, Washington Co., VT; d. 02 Mar 1990, Barre, Washington Co., VT.
- 48.   ii. CHARLES F. GALLAGHER, b. 02 Sep 1910, Barre, Washington Co., VT; d. 26 Oct 1990, Burlington, VT.
-   iii. LUCILLE R. GALLAGHER, b. 12 Mar 1912, Barre, Washington Co., VT.

29. MARY "MAMIE"[4] GALLAGHER *(MARTHA[3] MAHEDY, JANE[2] LECLAR, ANTHONY[1])* was born Jan 1887 in Barre, Washington Co., VT, and died in Quincy, Massachusetts. She married ARTHUR BALLOU. He was born Abt. 1885.

Child of MARY GALLAGHER and ARTHUR BALLOU is:
-   i. ARTHUR[5] BALLOU, b. 1912.

30. LUKE FRANCIS[3] GALLAGHER *(MARTHA[2] MAHEDY, JANE[1] LECLAR, ANTHONY[A])[7,8]* was born 01 Jan 1892 in Barre, Washington Co., VT[9,10]. He married, Abt. 1920 in Montpelior, VT, MAUDE A. GRIFFIN. She was born Abt. 1897 in Vermont.

Children of LUKE GALLAGHER and MAUDE GRIFFIN are:
  i.   LUKE G.[4] GALLAGHER, b. 1921, Barre, Washington Co., VT.
  ii. WILLIAM R. GALLAGHER, b. 1922, Barre, Washington Co., VT.
  iii. PATRICIA GALLAGHER, b. Barre, Washington Co., VT.

31. MARY E.[4] MAHEDY *(JAMES ALFRED[3], JANE[2] LECLAR, ANTHONY[1])* was born 09 Jun 1895 in Shefford, PQ, Canada, and died Sept. 1977 in Lawrence, Mass. She married, in 1918 in Massachusetts[147], LEO RAYMOND GUILFOYLE son of JAMES & ELIZABETH GUILFOYLE. He was born 31 Oct 1893 in Lawrence, Massachusetts[148,149]. In 1920 they lived in Leominster, Worcester Co., Mass. And in 1930 they were living in Kingston, Rockingham Co., NH.

Children of MARY MAHEDY and LEO GUILFOYLE are:
49.   i.   MARY F.[5] GUILFOYLE, b. 1920, Lawrence, Massachusetts.
50.   ii. MARJORIE A. GUILFOYLE, b. 05 Sep 1921, Leominster, Worcester Co., Massachusetts; d. 05 Dec 1992, Lawrence, Massachusetts.
51.   iii. LEONA E. GUILFOYLE, b. 1924, Lawrence, Massachusetts.

32. CLAYTON J.[4] DOWNS *(MARY JANE "JENNIE"[3] MAHEDY, JANE[2] LECLAR, ANTHONY[1])* was born 31 Mar 1899 in Leominster, Worcester Co., Massachusetts, and died 1946. CLAYTON married and had a son.

Child of CLAYTON DOWNS is:
  i.   JACK[5] DOWNS.

33. MARY MADELINE[4] DOWNS *(MARY JANE "JENNIE"*[3] *MAHEDY, JANE*[2] *LECLAR, ANTHONY*[1]*)* was born 24 May 1912 in Leominster, Worcester Co., Massachusetts, and died in Leominster, Worcester Co., Massachusetts. She married a DEWITT in Leominster, Worcester Co., Mass.. He was born Abt. 1910.

Child of MARY (DOWNS) DEWITT is:

     i.   CHILD[5] DEWITT, b. Leominster, Worcester Co., Massachusetts.

Generation No. 5

34. LEROY F.[5] DAVIS *(CALIFERNA[4] LECLAR, FERDINAND[3],*
JOHN BATTIS[2], ANTHONY[1]) was born 18 Jul 1890 in New York[151],
and died Dec 1973 in Ithaca, Tompkins Co., NY. He married
OLIVE E. Abt. 1915. She was born 1892 in New York. They lived
in Stittville, Oneida Co., NY and LEROY worked as a Heavy
Machinery Salesman.

Children of LEROY DAVIS and OLIVE E. are:

      i. HOWARD L.[6] DAVIS, b. Sep 1916, Oneida County,
      NY[152]; m. MARION AVARD, 11 Apr 1943, Rome,
      Oneida Co., NY. HOWARD served in the Air Force
      in WWII.

          Floyd, April 11, 1943
      Miss Avard Bride of Pvt. H. L. Davis

      Floyd, April 13 – Miss Marion Avard, daughter of Mr
      and Mrs. Jesse Avard, R. D. 4, Rome and Pvt. Howard L.
      Davis, son of Mr and Mrs. LeRoy Davis of this place were
      married at 1 o'clock on Sunday at the First Baptist Church
      Rome, by the Rev. David N. Boswell, pastor.

      The bride was given in marriage by her father. They
      were attended by Miss Velma Davis, Bristol, Va., sister of
      the bridegroom, and Earl Avard, brother of the bride.
      Ushers were Carl Davis, brother, and Herman Koenig.

      The bride was gowned in white brocaded satin made on
      princess ines with a sweetheart neck line, long sleeves and
      train. She wore a finger tip veil edged with wedding bells
      and carried a bouquet of gardenias.

      Miss Davis, maid of honor wore yellow brocaded
      organdy, a beaded tiara to match and carried a colonial
      bouquet of jonquils, peach gladiolas, pink roses and
      carnations with pink streamers.

      For traveling, the bride selected a beige tweed suit with
      green and brown accessories and wore a corsage of
      white roses.

      Mrs. Avard wore navy blue with white accessories
      and Mrs. Davis wore black crepe with trimmings of
      white. Both wore corsages of white gardenias.

After the ceremony, a reception was held at the home of the bride's parents. Relatives and friends were present from Oxford, Oneida, Utica, Rome, Holland Patent, Stittville and Floyd.

The couple are now visiting friends in Carthage. After a 15 - day furlough, Mr and Mrs. Davis will leave for California where they will reside. Mr. Davis is stationed at Muroc Air Base, Calif.

ii. LYNDON GARRY DAVIS, b. 27 Jun 1919, Oneida County, NY[153]; d. 17 Jul 1942.

Corp. Lyndon Davis Killed in Crash. Young Airplane Mechanic Victim of Accident in Trinidad.

Floyd, July 18, 1942 – Mr. and Mrs. LeRoy Davis received word Friday of the death of their son, Corp. Lyndon Garry Davis, which occurred in an airplane accident on July 17.

He was born June 27, 1919 at Holland Patent. He attended the Holland Patent High School from which he was graduated in 1939. He enlisted on Oct. 25, 1939 and was graduated from Roosevelt Field in airplane mechanics course in Oct. 1940. He was transferred to Panama in Nov. 1941, and later went to Trinidad where he has since been located.

Besides his parents he is survived by two brothers, Pvt. Howard Davis, Air Corps, Long Island; Carl Davis and one sister, Miss Velma Davis both at home; also his grandparents, Mr. and Mrs. Hugh Davis of Holland Patent.

iii.   CARL DAVIS, b. 1922, Oneida County, NY[154].

iv.   VELMA DAVIS, b. 1924, Oneida County, NY[154].

Harold E. Davis
(1892 – 1979)

35. HAROLD E.[5] DAVIS *(CALIFERNA[4] LECLAR, FERDINAND[3], JOHN BATTIS[2], ANTHONY[1])* was born 16 Aug 1892 in West Branch, New York[155], and died 29 Apr 1979 in Stittville, Oneida County, NY[156]. He married, in 1917, PEARL YERMAN[156]. She was born 1896 in New York[157], and died 04 May 1970 in Stittville, Oneida County, NY. HAROLD worked for Oneida County.

HAROLD & PEARL are buried in the Townsend Cemetery, Stittville, Oneida Co., NY.

Daily Sentinel, Rome
STITTVILLE -- Harold E. Davis, 86, of Mills St., former Town of Marcy highway superintendent and a retired employee of the county Department of Public Works, died Sunday, April 29, 1979, after being stricken near his home.

Born Aug. 16, 1892, in West Branch, he was the son of Hugh and Califerna LaClar Davis. He married Pearl Yerman in 1917 in Stittville. She died May 4, 1970.

Mr. Davis was a member of the United Methodist Church and a life member of the Stittville Fire Department.

Surviving are two daughters, Mrs. Clarence (Marjory) Herter, Ocala, Fla., and Mrs. Ambrose (Ruth) McDonald, Holland Patent; one son, Willard Davis, Rome; one sister, Mrs. David (Lula) Jones, Holland Patent; five grandchildren, and six great grandchildren.

Burial will be in Townsend Cemetery.

Children of HAROLD DAVIS and PEARL YERMAN are:

52. i. MILDRED G.[6] DAVIS, b. 27 Apr 1918, Stittville, Oneida County, NY; d. 25 May 1964, Utica, Oneida County, NY.

53. ii. RUTH M. DAVIS, b. 14 May 1920, Oneida County, NY; d. 10 Apr 2006, Holland Patent, Oneida, NY.

54. iii. MARJORIE E. DAVIS, b. 27 Aug 1922, Stittville, Oneida County, NY; d. 22 Jun 1981, Ocala, FL.

iv. BETTY E. DAVIS[159], b. 1925, Oneida County, NY; d. Bef. 1979.

v. WILLARD DAVIS, b. 17 Jul 1933, Oneida County, NY; d. Jun 1979, Rome, Oneida Co., NY.

Lula M. (Davis) Jones
(1897 – 1988)
Opposite Page

36. LULA M.⁵ DAVIS *(CALIFERNA⁴ LECLAR, FERDINAND³, JOHN BATTIS², ANTHONY¹)* was born Jul 1897 in New York[160], and died 1988. She married DAVID E. JONES[161] Abt. 1920 in Oneida County, New York. He was born 07 Oct 1893 in New York[162], and died Aug 1967 in Holland Patent, Oneida, NY.

Children of LULA DAVIS and DAVID JONES are:

55.	i.	DOROTHEA L.⁶ JONES, b. 12 May 1922, Oneida County, NY; d. Aug 1992, Holland Patent, Oneida, NY.
56.	ii.	CHARLOTTE JONES, b. 20 May 1931; d. 08 Jun 2002, Delmar, Albany, NY.

Jesse Ferdinand and Winifred H. (Lewis) LeClar
(1887 – 1975)   (1885 - 1974)

37. JESSE FERDINAND[5] LECLAR *(JOHN[4], FERDINAND[3], JOHN BATTIS[2], ANTHONY[1])[164]* was born 17 Aug 1887 in Oneida County, NY[165,166,167], and died 14 Apr 1975 in North Western, Oneida County, NY[168]. He married WINIFRED H. LEWIS 04 Dec 1907 in Presbyterian Manse, Holland Patent, Oneida County, NY[169], daughter of WILLIAM LEWIS and GRACE DAVIS. She was born 10 Sep 1885 in Western, Oneida County, New York, and died 15 Apr 1974 in North Western, Oneida County, NY. JESSE was a dairy farmer in Western, Oneida Co., NY.

Both JESSE and WINIFRED are buried in Westernville Cemetery, Westernville, Oneida Co., NY.

LeCLAR-LEWIS 1907

At the Presbyterian manse, Wednesday, December 4, at 7 p.m. by Rev. C. E. Fay, Jessie F. LeClar of North Western and Miss Winifred H. Lewis of Ava, were united in marriage. Leon O. Fox was best man and Miss Naomi M. Lewis, sister of the bride, bridesmaid.

The bride was prettily attired in a dove-colored traveling suit with hat to match. Mr. and Mrs. LeClar will reside at Northwestern, where Mr. LeClar is engaged in business as a miller.

Couple Marks 50th Wedding Anniversary

Mr. and Mrs. Jesse F. Le Clar, North Western residents who were married 50 years ago tomorrow, marked the occasion Sunday with an open house at their home, given by their children.

Mr. Le Clar and the former Winifred H. Lewis, Ava were married Dec 4, 1907 in the Presbyterian Manse, Holland Patent by the Rev. C. E. Fay.

Mrs. Le Clar is the daughter of the late Mr. and Mrs. William Lewis, Town of Western, and her husband the son of Mr. and Mrs. John Le Clar, also of Western.

The couple has two children, Mrs. Albert (Grace) Nestle, North Western, and Harold Le Clar, Big Brook and three grandsons, Rodney Nestle and Richard and Gerald Le Clar.

Among those at Sunday's observation were Mrs. Naomi Reams, North Western, sister of Mrs Le Clar, and Leon Fox, Westernville. They were attendants at the wedding.

OBITUARY --- April 16, 1974

NORTH WESTERN -- Mrs. Jesse F. LeClar, 88, of North Western, died Monday (April 15, 1974) at her home after a long illness.

The former Winifred Lewis, she was born in the Town of Western on Sept. 10, 1885, daughter of William and Grace Davis Lewis.

She was educated in the Webster Hill schools and was a lifelong resident of the Town of Western, living the last 36 years in North Western.

She was married in Holland Patent on Dec. 4, 1907.

Survivors are her husband, a daughter, Mrs. Albert (Grace) Nestle of North Western; a son, Harold J. LeClar of Westernville; three grandchildren, H. Richard LeClar of Westernville, Rodney A. Nestle of Verona and Gerald A. LeClar of Cooperstown; and two great-grandchildren.

Funeral services will be at 11 a.m. Thursday at her home with burial in Westernville Cemetery.

The family requests that those who wish to do so, make contributions to the North Western United Methodist memorial fund.

OBITUARY --- April 15, 1975

NORTH WESTERN --- Jesse F. LeClar, 87, a former Town of Western highway superintendent, died Monday (April 14, 1975) at the Rome Nursing Home after a long illness.

He was born in Western, Aug 17, 1887, son of John and Nellie Hogan LeClar. He and the former Winifred Lewis were married in Holland Patent Dec. 4, 1907. She died April 15, 1974.

He was formerly foreman for the county highway department, retiring in 1958. He had also at one time worked for the Law Bros. Construction Co.

He was a member and past trustee of the North Western United Methodist Church.

He leaves a daughter, Mrs. Albert (Grace) Nestle, Northwestern; a son, Harold J. LeClar, Westernville; a sister, Mrs. James (Nellie) Goodrich, Norwich; three grandchildren, Gerald A. LeClar of Cooperstown, Rodney N. Nestle of Verona, and H. Richard LeClar of Westernville; and two great-grandchildren.

Burial will be at the Westernville Cemetery at the convenience of the family.

Children of JESSE LECLAR and WINIFRED LEWIS are:

57.   i.   GRACE ELEANOR⁶ LECLAR, b. 19 Nov 1915,
            Western, Oneida County, New York; d. 04 Nov 2009,
            Rome, Oneida County, NY.
58.   ii. HAROLD JESSE LECLAR, b. 02 Aug 1918, Western,
            Oneida County, New York; d. 08 Sep 2000,
            Westernville, Oneida County, NY.

38. FLORENCE⁵ LECLAR *(JOHN⁴, FERDINAND³, JOHN BATTIS²,
ANTHONY¹)* was born 2 Oct 1888 in Oneida County, NY, and died
3 July 1917, of influenza, in Western, Oneida County, New York.
She married, 20 Nov 1907¹⁰⁰, LEON J. CUMMINGS, son of
WALTER J. & ELBA BURCH¹⁰⁰ CUMMINGS. He was born 14
June 1886 in New York, and died 2 June 1926 in Western, Oneida
County, New York.

LEON CUMMINGS married (2), 5 April 1920, ALICE J.
CAVANAUGH, born abt. 1892 in Rome, Oneida County, NY, the
daughter of GEORGE and ANNA CHANDLER CAVANAUGH.

FLORENCE, LEON, and ALICE are buried in the Westernville
Cemetery, Westernville, Oneida County, NY

*July 1917 --- The sympathy of the entire community goes out to the
Cummings and LeClare families in their sad affliction in the death of
their beloved Mrs. Florence LeClare Cummings, which occurred at an
early hour in the home of her parents, where she went a few weeks ago for
the benefit of her health. Mrs. Cummings lived when a child with her
parents on the Clark farm and a few years ago came back to live on a
farm purchased by her father-in-law, and it was here she lived when
stricken. She leaves three small children, her husband, parents and one
brother, Jesse LeClare of Western, one sister, Miss Nellie LeClare, who
lives at home. She was a member of the North Western M. E. Church,
but after coming to South Western she attended the church here, and was
a member of the ladies class in the Sunday School. Funeral services were
held yesterday at the home of her parents and at the M. E. Church of
Westernville, Rev. George Merritt officiating.*

NORTH WESTERN, June 3 (1926) --- At 11o'clock last night at his home here occurred the death of Leon James Cummings. He had been confined to his bed only ten days.

He was born at Hillside, June 14, 1886, and was the only child of Walter J. and the late Elba A. Burch Cummings. At Delta, by Rev. F. G. Curtis, Nov 20, 1907, he was married to Florence E. LeClar, who died July 3, 1917. By that union there were three children, Clayton, Doris and James, who survive.

In Rome, on April 5, 1920, by Rev. E. S. Pearce, he was united in marriage with Alice J. Cavanaugh, who survives with two sons, Clarence and Harley.

With the exception of one year in Marcy practically all his life had been spent in Western. He was a kind neighbor and always ready to help everyone.

Children of FLORENCE LECLAR and LEON CUMMINGS are:

59.   i.   CLAYTON LEON[6] CUMMINGS, b. 25 Dec 1908, Western, Oneida County, New York; d. 14 Jun 1988, Rome, Oneida County, NY.

    ii. DORIS MARJORIE CUMMINGS, b. 23 Jun 1910, Western, Oneida County, New York[177]; d. 23 Sep 1938, Rome, Oneida County, New York (never married)[177].

4 Generations.
Left-to-Right
Clayton Leon Cummings, John LeClar
Florence E. (LeClar) Cummings, Mary C. (Fox) LeClar

Doris M. Cummings

NORTH WESTERN - DORIS CUMMINGS DIES IN
ROME (1938) --- Miss Doris M. Cummings, 28, native of
the town of Western, died Friday, September 16, at her
home at Rome, after an illness of two weeks. She had been
in poor health for 12 years.

Miss Cummings was the daughter of the late Leon and
Florence LeClair Cummings and had resided in Rome for
the past twelve years. She attended the First M. E.
Church of Rome.

Surviving are her grandmother, Mrs. Nellie LeClair and
a brother, James, at home; a brother Clayton, two half-
brothers, Clarence and Harley, and her stepmother, Mrs.
Alice J. Cummings of North Western; an aunt, Mrs. James
Goodrich of Norwich; an uncle, Jesse F. LeClair of
Frenchville, and grandfather, Walter J. Cummings of
North Western.

The funeral was held from the Griffin & Aldrich funeral
parlors at 2:30 p.m., Monday. The bearers were Ernest
Evans, Howard Davis, James Van Dresar and Robert
Dodson.

The Rev. Mr. Dodge of the Calvary M. E. Church of
Rome officiated. Interment was at Westernville.

The esteem in which Miss Cummings was held by all
was testified by the many beautiful floral offerings which
filled the room and covered the casket.

The sympathy of this community is extended the family
in their bereavement.

James J. "Pete" and Beatrice (Pugh) Cummings

iii. JAMES JOHN "PETE" CUMMINGS, b. 09 Jan 1916, Western, Oneida County, New York[178]; m. (1) 10 Jan 1940; BEATRICE PUGH, b. May 9, 1913[178]; d. 29 Jan 1991, Oneida County, NY[178,179]; m. (2) 15 May 1993, Oneida County, NY[180] , ANNIE MCDONALD, b. Abt. 1923. PETE was a Corporal in the U.S. Army in WWII. He worked for Rome Mfg, and Revere for 40 years before retiring.

STEUBEN – March 19, 1940
   Mr. & Mrs. Fred Pugh announce the marriage of their daughter, Beatrice, to James J. Cummings of Rome on January 9, at Rome by the Rev. H. D. Holmes.

HOLLAND PATENT --- Beatrice P. Cummings, 77, of Steuben Street, died Tuesday, Jan 29, 1991, at St. Luke's Memorial Center, after a two month illness.

She was born May 9, 1913, in the Town of Steuben, the daughter of Fred and Mellie MacArthur Pugh. She was educated in Remsen schools and on Jan 10, 1940 she married James Cummings in Rome.

She was employed by the Oneida County Rural Telephone Company from 1952 until she retired in 1989.

She was a Presbyterian and member of the Loyal Order of the Moose in Rome.

Besides her husband, she is survived by two sisters, Mrs. Rachel Roberts, of Holland Patent, and Mrs. Maude Rizzo of Utica; four brothers, Willis and Byron, of Remsen, Percy, of West Edmeston, and Roy of Belleview, Fla.; two sisters-in-law, Mrs. Wellington (Hazel) Pugh, of Waterville, and Mrs. Raymond (Katherine) Pugh of Old Forge; several nieces and nephews.

The funeral will be 1 p.m Friday from the George W. Koerner Funeral Home, Holland Patent. Interment in Townsend Cemetery, Stittville, next spring.

In memory of Bea, donations may be made to the United Methodist Church of Steuben, Westernville, or North Western, the Prospect Ambulance or the Holland Patent Emergency Truck Fund.

James J. "Pete" and Annie (McDonald) Cummings
August 22, 2009
With the "Steuben Old Home Day Community Service Award"
"In Recognition and Appreciation of many years of Outstanding Service
to Steuben and the surrounding communities."

"Pete" and Annie were married May 15, 1993 in Holland Patent

McDonald - Cummings
Thirty-five friends and relatives of Annie and Pete Cummings Holland Patent held a horning to extend their best wishes to the couple on their recent marriage. An accordion, cow bells, school bells, and much noise was used to arouse the couple. Refreshments were served and fun was had by all.
Annie McDonald and Pete Cummings were united in marriage at St. Leo's Church on May 15, 1993.

Children of LEON CUMMINGS and ALICE CAVANAUGH are:

      iv. CLARENCE W.[2] CUMMINGS[13], b. 05 Mar 1921, Oneida County, NY[14]; d. Jun 1987, Boonville, Oneida County, NY[14].

59b.   v. HARLEY C. CUMMINGS, b. 19 May 1922, Oneida County, NY; d. 31 Aug 2001, Westernville, Oneida County, NY.

James Vernon & Nellie Hogan (LeClar) Goodrich
Edna Belle (standing) and Joyce Marie Goodrich

39. NELLIE HOGAN[5] LECLAR *(JOHN[4], FERDINAND[3], JOHN BATTIS[2], ANTHONY[1])* was born 21 Oct 1897 in Western, Oneida County, NY[181], and died 17 Apr 1988 in Norwich, Chenango County, New York[181]. She married, 24 May 1930 in Oneida County, NY, JAMES VERNON GOODRICH, JR.[182], son of JAMES V. GOODRICH and LENA B. ANDERSON. He was born 02 Aug 1901 in Norwich, Chenango County, New York[183], and died 08 Jan 1996 in Cumberland Center, Cumberland, ME[184]. JAMES worked for the O&W Railroad & for a grocery store in Norwich.

   Both NELLIE and JAMES are buried in Mt. Hope Cemetery, Plot: Section A Lot 724, Norwich, Chenango Co., NY.

NORWICH ---- Nellie Goodrich, 90, resident of the Valley View Manor Nursing Home of Norwich since February of 1984 and formerly of RD 1, Norwich, died April 17, 1988 at the home.

   She was born in Western New York and lived for many years in the Rome area until 1930, when she moved to Norwich. She had been a member of the Broad Street United Methodist Church of Norwich for over 50 years and had formerly been active in the Aldrich Bible Class as well as the Salamagundi Club.

   Born Oct. 21, 1897, in Western New York, she was a daughter of John and Nellie Hogan LeClar. On May 24, 1930, in Oneida, she married James V. Goodrich, who survives.

   Besides her husband, James V. Goodrich of Norwich, she is survived by two daughters, Mrs William (Joyce) Lawrence, Norwich, and Edna Beers, Wilder, Vt.; five grandchildren, Sgt. James Lawrence, stationed with the Army at Hinesville, Ga.; Jon Lawrence, Green Bay, Wisc.; William Lawrence, Norwich; Edward Beers Jr., San Diego, Cal.; and Andrew Beers, Albany; one niece, Grace Nestle, Rome; three nephews, Clayton Cummings, North Western; James Cummings, Holland Patent; and Harold LeClar, North Western; two great grandchildren, Alexander Lawrence and Jessica Lawrence, both of Hinesville, Ga.; and several cousins. She was predeceased by two sisters, Mabel LeClar and Florence Cummings, and by one brother, Jesse F. LeClar.

   Funeral services will be held at 1:30 p.m. Wednesday from the Fahy Funeral Home of Norwich. The Rev. George F. Goodwin, pastor of the Broad Street United Methodist Church of Norwich, will officiate. Burial will be at a later date in Mt. Hope Cemetery of Norwich.

Children of NELLIE LECLAR and JAMES GOODRICH are:
60.   i.   JOYCE MARIE[6] GOODRICH, b. 03 Jul 1931.
61.   ii.   EDNA BELLE GOODRICH, b. 20 Mar 1934, Norwich, Chenango County, New York.

40. JOHN F[5] WARCUP *(GERTRUDE "GERTIE" E.[4] LECLAR, FERDINAND[3], JOHN BATTIS[2], ANTHONY[1])* was born 10 Dec 1907 in Westernville, Oneida County, New York[185], and died 24 Dec 1975 in Rome Hospital, Rome, Oneida County, New York[185]. He married ELEANOR A. CORR 10 May 1941 in Westmoreland, Oneida Co., NY, daughter of WILLIAM J. CORR. She was born 05 Oct 1917, and died Mar 1986 in Rome, Oneida Co., NY. JOHN saw military service with the U.S. Army in WWII. Later, he worked for Texaco Oil Co.

J. F. WARCUP weds ELEANOR A. CORR
Marriage performed May 10 by Westmoreland Minister revealed.
   Miss Eleanor Corr, daughter of Mr. And Mrs. William J. Corr, Lee Center, and John F. Warcup, 327 Kosuth St., son of Frank and the late Gertie Warcup, were married May 10, it was announced today.
   The ceremony was performed by the Rev. George M. Pilbeam, pastor of the Westmoreland Methodist Church. Mr. and Mrs. George Reese, brother-in-law and sister of the bridegroom, were attendants.
   For her wedding, the bride wore an ensemble of navy blue wool crepe over night blue printed silk, with navy and white accessories. She wore a corsage of gardenias. Her attendant wore dusty pink crepe with white accessories. She had a corsage of Talisman roses.
   Both the bride and her husband attended Rome Free Academy, the latter being employed by the Z. & M. Oil Co. They are living at 327 Kossuth St.

Children of JOHN WARCUP and ELEANOR CORR are:
62.   i.   BRENDA[6] WARCUP.
       ii.   PATTY WARCUP, m. BRUCE BREMENT.

41. HAROLD OLIN[5] WARCUP (GERTRUDE "GERTIE" E.[4] LECLAR, FERDINAND[3], JOHN BATTIS[2], ANTHONY[1]) was born 20 Jun 1909 in Western, Oneida County, New York[186], and died 01 Jan 1983 in Western, Oneida County, New York[186]. He married ETHEL SLORAH[186] 1932, daughter of ELBERT SLORAH. She was born 18 Dec 1909[187], and died Jan 1989 in Sherrill, Oneida County, NY[187].

Nov. 2, 1944 - OES DEPUTY BEGINS WORK
ROME – *Mrs. Ethel S. Warcup, 612 W. Bloomfield, who was recently appointed district deputy grand matron of the Lewis-Oneida District, Order of the Eastern Star, has returned after attending a reception in Ogdensburg for Nellie M. Rutherford, grand matron of the OES in New York state.*

Mrs. Warcup was matron of Lake Delta Chapter, OES, Lee Center in 1939. She is the wife of Harold O. Warcup, past patron of Lake Delta Chapter 590, and past master of Baron Steuben Lodge, F&AM.

She is a daughter of Mr. and Mrs. Elbert Slorah, Steuben, is a native of Steuben and a graduate of Holland Patent High School and the Excelsior School of Business. Since 1928, she has been secretary to the Oneida County district superintendents of schools whose offices are in the Court House at Utica. She is active in Parent-Teacher Association activities in Rome.

CELEBRATE GOLDEN
Mr. and Mrs. Harold O. Warcup, 225 E. Noyes Blvd, Sherrill, formerly of 612 W. Bloomfield st., were honored by their children at a 50th wedding anniversary party at Karrat's Restaurant. Mr. Warcup formerly owned a fuel oil business, and Mrs Warcup is a retired employee of the Vernon-Verona-Sherrill school district. The couple has two grandchildren.

OBITUARY
Harold O. Warcup, 73, or 122 Barefoot Trail, Port Orange, Fla, and 225 Noyes Blvd, Sherrill, former owner of H. O. Warcup Oil Co., died Saturday, Jan 1, 1983, in Daytona Community Hospital, Daytona Beach, Fla.

Born in Westernville on June 20, 1909, he was the son of Frank and Gertie LeClar Warcup. In 1932, he married Ethel Slorah.

A 1927 graduate of Rome Free Academy, he attended Rochester Institute of Technology. For several years he was employed by Mobil Oil Co. before forming H. O. Warcup Oil Co. Later, he was associated with Nolan, Hayes, and Warcup Oil Co. After his retirement, he was employed by the Vernon - Verona - Sherrill school system.

Mr. Warcup was a member of Christ Church United Methodist, Sherrill. He was past master of Steuben Masonic Lodge; past patron of the Lake Delta Chapter of the Order of the Eastern Star, Lee Center; right worthy grand director of ceremonies of the . . . Utica Patrol, and a member of the Scottish Rite, Utica, and Ziyara Shrine, Utica.

Surviving besides his wife are a son, Howard Warcup, Franklin, Mass.; two daughters, Linda Warcup, Rome, and Sandra Warcup, Clearwater, Fla.; a sister Mrs. Arthur (Florence) Walsworth, Westernville, and two grandchildren.

A local memorial service will be held in the spring with burial in Westernville Cemetery.

Children of HAROLD WARCUP and ETHEL SLORAH are:

    i.   HOWARD JOHN[6] WARCUP, b. 10 Dec 1932, Oneida County, NY; d. 26 Apr 2000, Ashville, NC; m. ELOISE BROWN, 01 Oct 1960, Churchville, Oneida Co., NY;

Aug. 1960 – Wedding Announcement

Miss Eloise Brown, Rochester, daughter of the Rev. Walter M. Brown, Leechburg, Pa., and the late Mrs. Brown, to Howard John Warcup, Churchville, formerly of Rome, son of Mr. And Mrs. Harold O. Warcup, 612 W. Bloomfield St., Rome.

Miss Brown was graduated from Roberts Wesleyan College, North Chili. Her fiance is a graduate of the Bentley School of Accounting, Boston, Mass., where he was a member of Kappa Pi Alpha fraternity.

Miss Brown is employed by the Taylor Instrument Co., and Mr. Warcup is with the Joseph Harris Seed Co., Rochester.

The wedding will take place Oct. 1 in Churchville.

   ii.   LINDA WARCUP, b. Oneida County, NY. In 1983 she lived in Rome, Oneida County, New York.

  iii.   SANDRA ELAINE WARCUP, b. Abt. 1949, Oneida County, NY.

42. CHARLES BROOKS. F.[5] GIBBS *(JOSEPHINE[4] FLINT, MARY ANN[3] LECLAR, JOHN BATTIS[2], ANTHONY[1])* was born 27 Sep 1894 in Jefferson County, NY[105,106] and died 02 Aug 2000 in Rochester, Monroe Co., NY. He married BLANCHE HAYNES, 29 Aug 1921. She was born 05 Feb 1899 in New York and died 29 Oct 1998 in Rochester, NY. CHARLES attended Syracuse University. He was a Physician in Rochester, NY.

Child of CHARLES GIBBS and BLANCHE HAYNES is:
    i.   NANCY JANE[7] GIBBS, b. 18 Jun 1926, Rochester, Monroe Co. NY.

43. DR. ROBERT FLINT D.[5] GIBBS *(JOSEPHINE[4] FLINT, MARY ANN[3] LECLAR, JOHN BATTIS[2], ANTHONY[1])* was born 05 Mar 1898 in Jefferson County, NY, and died Mar 1975 in Seneca Falls, NY. He married DOROTHY E. HASLOCK, 17 June 1926. She was born 27 Aug 1905 in New York, and died Mar 1986 in Seneca Falls, NY. ROBERT GIBBS was a Physician in Seneca Falls, NY.

Child of ROBERT and DOROTHY GIBBS is:
    i.   ROBERT FLINT[7] GIBBS, b. Jul 1928, Seneca Falls, NY.

44. RAYMOND ROBERT[5] RUHM *(MARY C.[4] BARNES, SARAH JANE[3] BUTLER, MARY A.[2] LECLAR, ANTHONY[1])* was born 14 Apr 1893 in Munnsville, Madison County, New York, and died 13 Jun 1954. He married GERTRUDE A. abt. 1917 in Oneida County, New York. She was born 1898 in New York.

    Although identified, in the 1900 census and on his WWI draft registration card, as RAYMOND ROBERT RUHM, he seemed to prefer to go by the name ROBERT. He lived for a short time in Springfield, Mass. Where he registered for the draft for WWI and worked as a machinist.

Child of RAYMOND ROBERT and GERTRUDE A. RUHM is:
63.   i.   ROBERT RAYMOND[7] RUHM, JR., b. 19 Jun 1919, Utica, Oneida County, NY; d. 21 Jan 2009, Utica, Oneida County, NY.

45. FRANCES M.[5] RUHM *(MARY C[4] BARNES, SARAH JANE[3] BUTLER, MARY A.[2] LECLAR, ANTHONY[1])* was born 27 Jun 1896 in New York; d. Feb 1983 in Houston, Texas. She married RALPH BABBITT BENEDICT, 02 Feb 1918. He was born 04 Mar 1893 in Unadilla Flats, Otsego County, NY, and died 17 Oct 1965 in Connecticut.

Child of FRANCES RUHM and RALPH BENEDICT is:
    i.   VIRGINIA[7] BENEDICT, b. 1923, Utica, Oneida County, NY.

46. DOROTHY G.[5] OPPER *(CHARLES M. 'CHARLIE'[4], MARTHA ANN[3] REYNOLDS, SARAH[2] LECLAR, ANTHONY[1])*[200,201] was born 1905 in Ava, Oneida, NY, and died 27 Mar 1962 in Rome, Oneida, NY[202]. She married HOLLIS B. HURLBUT Abt. 1926 in Ava, Oneida County, NY, son of BURTON S. & SATIE HURLBUT. He was born 1905, and died 18 Mar 1989.

    DOROTHY and HOLLIS are buried in the Ava Cemetery, Ava, Oneida Co., NY.

Utica Daily Press - March 28, 1962

    Mrs. Dorothy O. Hurlbut, 56, wife of Hollis Hurlbut, died yesterday in Rome City Hospital.

    She was born at Ava, daughter of Charles M. and Beatrice Kilts Opper. She attended Boonville High School and later studied home economics at Morrisville Agricultural and Technical Institute.

    She was married to Hollis Hurlbut at Ava. After their marriage they resided in Rome. Later they purchased the Dewey Adams farm, Ava, where they resided until 10 years ago when they came here. Mrs. Hurlbut was a member of Ava Methodist Church and its Ladies Aid Society.

    Besides her husband, she leaves a daughter, Mrs. Jospeh P. Felice, of Lockport, two brothers, Norman W. Opper, of Ava, Donald K. Opper of Rome.

Child of DOROTHY OPPER and HOLLIS HURLBUT is:
    i.   MARTHA BEATRICE[6] HURLBUT, b. 1928; m. JOSEPH P. FELICE; b. 13 Nov 1920[203]; d. 28 Nov 2005[203]. JOSEPH saw service as a S/SGT in the U.S. Army in WWII. He is buried in the Ava Cemetery, Ava, Oneida Co., NY

Hurlbuts hold reunion - Aug 2009
The descendents of Burton and Satie Hurlbut held their
annual reunion on Aug. 16 at the home of Keith and
Nancy King of Rome, with 30 family members and guests
in attendance.
Brennan Emanuelli, 2-year-old son of Todd and Kristin
King-Emanuelli of Rome, was the youngest in attendance.
The oldest was Myrtle Milles, 89, of Rome.
Traveling the farthest to attend was **Martha Felice**, *of*
St. Petersburg, Fla.

47. LEO R.[5] GALLAGHER *(CHARLES RICHARD[4], MARTHA[3]*
MAHEDY, JANE[2] LECLAR, ANTHONY[1]) was born 09 Aug 1908 in
Barre, Washington Co., VT[204], and died 02 Mar 1990 in Barre,
Washington Co., VT[204]. He married OLIVE LEFEBRE 16 Dec 1939
in Barre, Washington Co., VT. She was born 15 Apr 1921[204], and
died 26 Apr 1994 in Barre, Washington Co., VT[204].

Children of LEO GALLAGHER and OLIVE LEFEBRE are:
  i. CHILD1[6] GALLAGHER, b. Abt. 1941, Barre,
     Washington Co., VT.
  ii. CHILD2 GALLAGHER, b. Abt. 1943, Barre,
     Washington Co., VT.
  iii. CHILD3 GALLAGHER, b. Abt. 1945, Barre,
     Washington Co., VT.
  iv. GEORGE GALLAGHER, b. 21 Mar 1947, Barre,
     Washington Co., VT; d. 29 Aug 1967 in Danang,
     Vietnam, while serving with the U.S. Navy as a
     Hospitalman.
  v. CHILD5 GALLAGHER, b. Abt. 1949, Barre,
     Washington Co., VT.

48. CHARLES F.[5] GALLAGHER *(CHARLES RICHARD[4],*
MARTHA[3] MAHEDY, JANE[2] LECLAR, ANTHONY[1]) was born 02
Sep 1910 in Barre, Washington Co., VT[204], and died 26 Oct 1990 in
Burlington, VT[204]. He married STELLA ANGUS 17 Jun 1944. She
was born Abt. 1920.

Children of CHARLES GALLAGHER and STELLA ANGUS are:
- i.   CHILDa[6] GALLAGHER, b. Abt. 1946, Barre, Washington Co., VT.
64. - ii. GEORGE D. GALLAGHER, b. 03 Jan 1948, Barre, Washington Co., VT; d. 1993, Lebanon, NH.
- iii. CHILDc GALLAGHER, b. Abt. 1950, Barre, Washington Co., VT.
- iv. CHILDd GALLAGHER, b. Abt. 1952, Barre, Washington Co., VT.

49. MARY F.[5] GUILFOYLE *(MARY E.[4] MAHEDY, JAMES ALFRED[3], JANE[2] LECLAR, ANTHONY[1])* was born 1920 in Lawrence, Massachusetts. She married MICHAEL F. SULLIVAN 1948 in Lawrence, Massachusetts. He was born 25 Apr 1915, and died 25 Feb 1988 in Lawrence, Massachusetts.

MARY GUILFOYLE and MICHAEL SULLIVAN had two children born in Lawrence, Massachusetts.

50. MARJORIE A.[5] GUILFOYLE *(MARY E.[4] MAHEDY, JAMES ALFRED[3], JANE[2] LECLAR, ANTHONY[1])* was born 05 Sep 1921 in Leominster, Worcester Co., Massachusetts, and died 05 Dec 1992 in Lawrence, Massachusetts. She married RONALD CLAMP 01 Mar 1944 in Lawrence, Massachusetts. He was born 22 Jan 1920[204], and died 20 Feb 1999[204].

 MARJORIE GUILFOYLE and RONALD CLAMP had two children born in Lawrence, Massachusetts.

51. LEONA E.[5] GUILFOYLE *(MARY E.[4] MAHEDY, JAMES ALFRED[3], JANE[2] LECLAR, ANTHONY[1])* was born 1924 in Lawrence, Massachusetts. She married STEVEN O'DONOHUE 1947 in Lawrence, Massachusetts. He was born Abt. 1920.

LEONA GUILFOYLE and STEVEN O'DONOHUE had six children born in Lawrence, Massachusetts.

Generation No. 6

52. MILDRED G.[6] DAVIS *(HAROLD E.[5], CALIFERNA[4] LECLAR, FERDINAND[3], JOHN BATTIS[2], ANTHONY[1])*[205,206] was born 27 Apr 1918 in Stittville, Oneida County, NY[207,207], and died 25 May 1964 in Utica, Oneida County, NY. She married FREDERICK L. KIRK 29 Jun 1946 in Rome, Oneida Co., NY. He was born Abt. 1918.

Stittvile woman, 46, passes away.
Mrs. Mildred G. Kirk, 46, wife of Frederick L. Kirk, died Monday in St. Luke's Memorial Hospital Center, Utica.
Daughter of Harold and Pearl Yerman Davis, she was born in Stittville, April 27, 1918, and was educated in the Holland Patent schools.
She was married to Mr. Kirk on June 29, 1946 at St. Mary's Church, Rome.
Mrs. Kirk was a member of St. Leo's Church, Holland Patent.
Besides her husband, she leaves her parents in Stittville; two daughters, Joan Marie and Cheryl Ann, both at home; two sisters, Mrs. Ruth Fear, Stittville, and Mrs. Clarence Herter, Rome, and one brother, Willard Davis, Stittville.

Children of MILDRED DAVIS and FREDERICK KIRK are:
     i.   JOAN MARIE[7] KIRK.
    ii.   CHERYL ANN KIRK.

53. RUTH M.[6] DAVIS *(HAROLD E.[5], CALIFERNA[4] LECLAR, FERDINAND[3], JOHN BATTIS[2], ANTHONY[1])*[207] was born 14 May 1920 in Oneida County, NY, and died 10 Apr 2006 in Holland Patent, Oneida, NY. She married (1) NORMAN FEAR Abt. 1940. He was born Abt. 1920. She married (2) AMBROSE MCDONALD Abt. 1960. He was born 05 Jun 1921 in New York, and died 13 Aug 2006 in Holland Patent, Oneida, NY.

Children of RUTH DAVIS and NORMAN FEAR are:
     i.   STEVE[7] FEAR, m. (1) SHEILA SANDER; m. (2) LINDA NASH.
65.   ii.   SUSAN FEAR.

54. MARJORIE E.[6] DAVIS *(HAROLD E.[5], CALIFERNA[4] LECLAR, FERDINAND[3], JOHN BATTIS[2], ANTHONY[1])[207]* was born 27 Aug 1922 in Stittville, Oneida County, NY, and died 22 Jun 1981 in Ocala, FL[208]. She married (1) DANIEL C. SEXTON Abt. 1940. He was born Abt. 1920, and died 17 Nov 1944 in France. She married (2) CLARENCE M. HERTER 18 Aug 1951. He was born 10 Nov 1897[208], and died Nov 1985 in Ocala, FL[208]. DANIEL C. SEXTON graduated in 1939 from Holland Patent Central School, and graduated in 1940 from the Utica School of Commerce. He was a member of the Stittville Fire Department. He was serving with the U.S. Army during WWII when he was killed in France.

Both MARJORIE and CLARENCE HERTER are buried in Evergreen Cemetery, Lee, Oneida Co., NY.

Children of MARJORIE DAVIS and DANIEL SEXTON are:
       i.   HAROLD[7] SEXTON[209], b. Abt. 1941.
      ii.   ARTHUR SEXTON[210], b. Abt. 1942.

55. DOROTHEA L.[6] JONES *(LULA M.[5] DAVIS, CALIFERNA[4] LECLAR, FERDINAND[3], JOHN BATTIS[2], ANTHONY[1])[211]* was born 12 May 1922 in Oneida County, NY[212,213], and died Aug 1992 in Holland Patent, Oneida, NY[213]. She married JOSEPH WILLIAMS[214]. He was born in 1916 in New York[215], and died 15 Feb 2009 in Holland Patent, Oneida, NY[215].

Child of DOROTHEA JONES and JOSEPH WILLIAMS is:
66.   i.   JOANN[7] WILLIAMS, b. 1952.

56. CHARLOTTE[6] JONES *(LULA M.[5] DAVIS, CALIFERNA[4] LECLAR, FERDINAND[3], JOHN BATTIS[2], ANTHONY[1])* was born 20 May 1931[215], and died 08 Jun 2002 in Delmar, Albany, NY[215]. She married HOWARD D. AUSTIN. He was born 08 Feb 1921[215], and died 26 Jan 2010 in Delmar, Albany, NY[215].

Children of CHARLOTTE JONES and HOWARD AUSTIN are:
67.   i.   HOWARD[7] AUSTIN, b. 1956.
68.   ii.   STEVEN AUSTIN, b. 1957.
69.   iii. ANDREW AUSTIN, b. 1960.
70.   iv. TIMOTHY AUSTIN, b. 1961.
71.   v.   JULIE AUSTIN, b. 1964.

Albert F. & Grace Eleanor (LeClar) Nestle.
(1941 Wedding photo – on left)
Harold & Audra LeClar (on right)

57. GRACE ELEANOR[6] LECLAR *(JESSE FERDINAND[5], JOHN[4], FERDINAND[3], JOHN BATTIS[2], ANTHONY[1])* was born 19 Nov 1915 in Western, Oneida County, New York[216], and died 04 Nov 2009 in Rome, Oneida County, NY[216]. She married ALBERT F. NESTLE[217,218] 06 Dec 1941 in Hallstead, Pennsylvania[219], son of GEORGE HENRY NESTLE and MARGARET GRABNER. He was born 31 Mar 1903 in Western, Oneida County, New York[220], and died 23 Jul 1978 in North Western, Oneida County, NY[220].

North Western, Dec 9, 1941
   The marriage of Miss Grace Le Clar, only daughter of Mr. and Mrs. Jesse Le Clar of Frenchville, and Albert Nestle, son of Mr. and Mrs. George Nestle of Westernville, took place at noon Saturday at Hallstead, Pa., with Fred C. W. Carl officiating. They were attended by Mr. and Mrs. Harold Le Clar, brother and sister-in-law of the bride.
   The bride was attired in a soldier blue silk crepe street length dress with navy accessories and wore a corsage of talisman roses and delphiniums. The matron of honor wore a street length dress of moss green silk crepe with brown accessories and a corsage of pink roses and delphiniums.
   After the ceremony the couple returned to Barnard Hall, North Western, where a reception was held fro friends and relatives with Mrs. William Dudley as cateress and the Misses Marian and Dorothy Davis as waitresses. Tables were decorated with pink and white and a bride's cake.
   The bride is employed at Rome State School and the bridegroom is employed in the rolling mill at Revere.

NORTH WESTERN – July 1978
   Albert F. Nestle, 75, of 9944 Main St., died Sunday, July 23, 1978, at home. He was a retired patrol foreman for the state Department of Transportation.
   Born March 31, 1903 in Westernville, he was the son of George and Margaret Grabner Nestle. He attended Westernville schools.
   On Dec 7, 1941 (should be Dec 6) he married Grace LeClair in Pennsylvania. He resided in North Western for the past 33 years.
   Mr. Nestle was formerly employed by the Olney and Floyd Co., Westernville, and Revere Copper and Brass, Rome. He was a member of North Western Methodist Church and the Volunteer Fire Department.

Surviving besides his wife are two sons, Albert F. Nestle, Jr., Oswego, and Rodney Nestle, Verona; five sisters, Mrs. Donald (Frances) Meeker, North Western; Mrs. Rachel Button, Syracuse; Mrs. Audrey Pugh, Floyd; Mrs. Edna Fahy, Rome, and Mrs. Donald (Violet) Abduhl, Verona Mills; three brothers, Henry Nestle, North Western, Foster Nestle and Robert Nestle, Westernville, and 10 grandchildren.

Funeral services will be at 1:30 p.m. at Prince and Boyd funeral home. Burial will be in Westernville Cemetery.

OBITUARY - Grace E. Nestle

Grace E. Nestle, 93, of South James St., Rome, formerly of North Western, died Wednesday, November 4, 2009 at St. Elizabeth Hospital. She was born November 19, 1915 in the Town of Western, the daughter of Jesse F. and Winifred Lewis LeClar. She attended Westernville schools and graduated from Rome Free Academy. On December 7, 1941, she married Albert F. Nestle in Pennsylvania. He died July 23, 1978. Grace had worked at the Rome State School, Oneida County Home, Rome Memorial Hospital and also private home health care. She was a member of the North Western United Methodist Church.

She is survived by a son and daughter-in-law, Rodney and Patricia Nestle, Verona; and a grandson, Rodney Nestle Jr. and his wife Denise, Verona; a cousin, James "Pete" Cummings and his wife Annie, Holland Patent; two nephews, Harold "Dick" and Joyce LeClar, Boonville, and Gerald and Gerry LeClar, Oxford, N.Y.; and a close friend, John Westcott, Taberg. She was predeceased by a brother and sister-in-law, Harold and Audra LeClar.

Funeral services will be held at Prince-Boyd & Hyatt Home for Funerals, Inc., 210 W. Court St., Rome, Friday at 2 p.m. with the Rev. Robert Wollaber officiating. Interment will be in Westernville Cemetery. Relatives and friends may call at the home for funerals Friday from 12-2 p.m. Memorial contributions may be made to the Rome Humane Society, P.O. Box 4572, Rome, N.Y. 13442.

Child of GRACE LECLAR and ALBERT NESTLE is:

72.   i.   RODNEY ALBERT[7] NESTLE, b. 28 Sep 1943, Oneida County, NY.

July 4, 1940 Wedding Photo
Harold Jesse LeClar & Audra Minnie Meeker

Attendants: Grace LeClare & Albert Nestle

81

Harold Jesse & Audra Minnie (Meeker) LeClar

58. HAROLD JESSE[6] LECLAR *(JESSE FERDINAND[5], JOHN[4], FERDINAND[3], JOHN BATTIS[2], ANTHONY[1])* was born 02 Aug 1918 in Western, Oneida County, New York, and died 08 Sep 2000 in Westernville, Oneida County, NY[223]. He married AUDRA MINNIE MEEKER 04 Jul 1940[224], daughter of JERRY C. MEEKER and RUBY HILL. She was born 21 Jul 1918 in Steuben, Oneida County, NY, and died 28 Sep 2004 in Westernville, Oneida County, NY[225].

HAROLD JESSE LECLAR and AUDRA MINNIE MEEKER are buried in the Carmichael Hill Cemetery, Oneida County, NY

OBITUARY
Westernville --- Harold J. LeClar, 82, of 9481 Long Shore Road, died Friday, sept 8, 2000 at Rome Memorial Hospital.
He was born August 2, 1918 in the Town of Western the son of Jesse F. and Winifred Lewis LeClar.
Harold graduated from Rome Free Academy in 1936.
On July 4, 1940 he married Audra M. Meeker in Westmoreland United Methodist Parsonage by the Rev. George Pilbeam.
Harold was a cattle dealer and trucker retiring in 1983.
Mr. LeClar was a member and trustee of Steuben United Methodist Church, Charter member and past president of Volunteer Fire Department of Western, Fifty year member of Steuben Grange and a member of the executive committee, Steuben Senior Citizens, and the Historical Society of Western.
In 1995 Harold received Citizen of the Year Award from the Steuben Old Home Days Association.
He is survived by his wife Audra and two sons and daughters -in-law, Harold (Dick) and Joyce LeClar of Boonville and Gerald and Gerry LeClar of Oxford. One sister Grace Nestle of Rome. Three grandchildren Susan LeClar, Nadine and Chris LeClar; a brother-in-law and sister-in-law George and Betty Meeker, Florida. A special cousin James (Pete) Cummings and his wife Annie, Holland Patent, and several nieces and nephews.
Funeral services will be held at the Steuben United Methodist Church, Monday at 1 p.m. Burial will be in Carmichael Hill Cemetery. . . . Memorial contributions may be made to the Steuben United Methodist Church or the Volunteer Fire Department of Western.

OBITUARY

Audra Meeker LeClar, 86, of 9481 Long Shore Road, died Tuesday, September 28, 2004 at Rome Memorial Hospital. She was born July 21, 1918 in the Town of Steuben, daughter of Jerry C. and Ruby Hill Meeker. She graduated from Holland Patent High School in 1934 and attended Excelsior School of Business in Utica. On July 4, 1940 she was married to Harold J. LeClar in the Westmoreland Methodist Parsonage by the Rev. George Pilbeam. Harold died September 8, 2000.

Audra was employed by the law office of Griffith & Pileckas and retired from Emlyn I. Griffith Law Office in 1984 after 22 years. She was a member and trustee of the Steuben United Methodist Church, president of Steuben United Methodist Women's Society and for many years was superintendent and Sunday School Teacher in Steuben. Audra was a 72 year member of the Steuben Grange 1471 and served as master, chaplain and presently as lecturer. She was a member of the Oneida County Pomona Grange and served as Drill Master or Degree Team for several years. She was also a member of the New York State and National Granges.

In 1991 she received the Oneida County Granger of the Year and in 1995 Audra and Harold received the Grange Couple of the Year, and in 2003 she was awarded the Gerald Eastman Award for Outstanding Community Service given by New York State Grange.

She was a member of both Remsen-Steuben and Town of Western Historical Societies, Director of Steuben and Carmichael Hill Cemeteries and was a member of the Steuben Seniors. Audra was a member of the executive committee of Steuben Old Home Days and for many years served as chairperson of the annual dinner. In 1990 she received the Community Service Award for years of dedicated service to Steuben and surrounding communities from the Steuben Old Home Days Association. Audra also had a great love for gardening.

She is survived by two sons and daughters-in-law, Harold (Dick) and Joyce LeClar, Boonville, and Gerald and Gerry LeClar of Oxford; one brother and sister-in-law, George and Betty Meeker, Avon Park, Fla.; three grandchildren, Susan LeClar, Boonville, Nadine Kneale and her husband Tim, of New Berlin and Chris LeClar, Lawrenceville, Ga.; and one great-grandson Brandon Kneale; one sister-in-law, Grace Nestle, Rome; and several nieces and nephews.

The family would like to thank neighbors and friends for their care and thoughtfulness for mother. Funeral services will be held at the Steuben United Methodist Church Saturday at 11 a.m. Burial will be in Carmichael Hill Cemetery.

Memorial contributions may be made to Steuben United Methodist Church or Carmichael Hill Cemetery Association.

Children of HAROLD LECLAR and AUDRA MEEKER are:
73.   i.   HAROLD RICHARD "DICK"[7] LECLAR, b. 13 Sep 1942, Rome, Oneida County, NY.
74.   ii. GERALD ALLEN "JERRY" LECLAR, b. 08 Jun 1949, Oneida County, NY.

Wedding Photo – December 8, 1941
Clayton Leon Cummings & Ethel E. Evans

Attendants (on each side)
Beatrice (Pugh) Cummings & James "Pete" Cummings

59. CLAYTON LEON⁶ CUMMINGS *(FLORENCE E.⁵ LECLAR, JOHN⁴, FERDINAND³, JOHN BATTIS², ANTHONY¹)* was born 25 Dec 1908 in Western, Oneida County, New York, and died 14 Jun 1988 in Rome, Oneida County, NY. He married ETHEL E. EVANS 08 Dec 1941 in Steuben, Oneida County, NY[226], daughter of JOHN EVANS and JANE ELLIS. She was born 29 Sep 1912 in Vernon, Oneida County, NY, and died 18 Jan 2002 in Rome, Oneida County, NY.

Steuben - **Cummings-Evans**
  Steuben, Dec 11 (1941) -- Miss Ethel E. Evans of Remsen, formerly of Steuben, daughter of Mrs Jane Evans and the late John Evans, became the bride of Clayton L. Cummings of North Western Monday evening at the Steuben parsonage, the Rev. A. R. Meyers, officiating.
  The bride wore a sailor blue dress with blue accessories and a corsage of white roses. The attendants were Mr. and Mrs. James Cummings of Rome. Mrs. Cummings wore cloud blue with black accessories and a corsage of pink roses.
  Mrs. Cummings had resided in Steuben until about two years ago when the family moved to Remsen. She was a member of the Steuben Methodist Church and sang in the church choir. She is a graduate of the Rome Free Academy.
  They will reside in North Western where the bridegroom has employment.

OBITUARY - North Western - Clayton L. Cummings, 79, of Mill Street, a heavy equipment operator for 30 years at Griffis Air Force Base before retiring in 1974, died Tuesday, June 14, 1988, in Rome Hospital, where he had been a patient since June 9.
  Born on Dec 25, 1908, in the Town of Western, he was a son of Leon and Florence LeClar Cummings. He married Ethel Evans, in Steuben, on Dec 8, 1941. He was a member of North Western United Methodist Church.
  Surviving besides his wife, are a son, Gary W. Cummings, Holland Patent; two brothers, James "Pete" Cummings, Holland Patent, and Harley Cummings, North Western; and two grandchildren.
  Services will be at 11 a.m. Friday at Prince-Boyd and Hyatt Funeral Home, Rome. Burial will be in Westernville Cemetery. Calling hours are from 7 to 9 tonight, and from 2 to 4 and 7 to 9 p.m. Thursday. Donations may be made to the North Western United Methodist Church.

OBITUARY

Ethel E. Cummings, 89, formerly of Mill Street, North Western and recently of Holland Patent died Friday, January 18, 2002 at Rome Memorial Hospital after a long illness. She was born September 29, 1912 in Vernon, N.Y. one of eleven children of John and Jane Evans. She attended Steuben schools and graduated from Rome Free Academy. On December 8, 1941 she married Clayton L. Cummings. He died June 14, 1988. She was a very active member of the North Western United Methodist Church and was also a member of the North Western Senior Citizens.

She is survived by one son and daughter-in-law, Gary W. and Carol Cummings, Holland Patent; two sisters, Margaret Oliver, Rome and Ruth Ingersol, Remsen; two grandchildren, Kathy Beckerman and her husband Adam, and Lance Cummings and his wife Melissa; and two great-grandchildren, Michael and Max; a brother-in-law, James "Pete" Cummings and his wife Annie, Holland Patent; and a sister-in-law, Barbara Cummings, North Western.

The family would like to thank Hospice for their wonderful care and a a special thank you to nieces, Janet, Mary and Alice.

Funeral services will be held at the Prince-Boyd & Hyatt Home for Funerals, Inc., Saturday at 5 p.m. Spring internment will be in Westernville Cemetery. Relatives and friends may call at the home for funerals Saturday from 2-5 p.m. Memorial contributions may be made to Hospice Care, Inc or the North Western United Methodist Church.

Child of CLAYTON CUMMINGS and ETHEL EVANS is:
75.   i.   GARY W.[7] CUMMINGS, b. 09 Oct 1945.

59b. HARLEY C. CUMMINGS was born 19 May 1922 in Oneida County, NY[16], and died 31 Aug 2001 in Westernville, Oneida County, NY[16]. He married, 13 Jul 1957 in the Methodist Church, Westernville, Oneida Co., NY, BARBARA LAQUAY. BARBARA was born 27 Sep 1930 and died 21 Jan 2003.   HARLEY served in the U.S. Army in both WWII and Korea.

Child of HARLEY CUMMINGS and BARBARA LAQUAY is:
        i.   CARLISLE CUMMINGS, m. RICHARD KONIK.

60. JOYCE MARIE[6] GOODRICH *(NELLIE HOGAN[5] LECLAR, JOHN[4], FERDINAND[3], JOHN BATTIS[2], ANTHONY[1])* was born 03 Jul 1931. She married WILLIAM CHARLES LAWRENCE[227] 13 Jan 1951 in Broad Street Methodist Church, Norwich, NY. He was born 19 Oct 1929[228].

Children of JOYCE GOODRICH and WILLIAM LAWRENCE are:
76. i. JAMES WILLIAM[7] LAWRENCE, b. 13 Oct 1951, Norwich, Chenango County, New York.
     ii. JON MICHAEL LAWRENCE, b. 27 May 1954, Norwich, Chenango County, New York; m. MELISSA MARIE BARRETT; b. 1968. In 1988 JON MICHAEL lived in Green Bay, Wisconsin.
     iii. WILLIAM CHARLES LAWRENCE, JR., b. 25 Apr 1961, Norwich, Chenango County, New York.

61. EDNA BELLE[6] GOODRICH *(NELLIE HOGAN[5] LECLAR, JOHN[4], FERDINAND[3], JOHN BATTIS[2], ANTHONY[1])* was born 20 Mar 1934 in Norwich, Chenango County, New York. She married EDWARD RAYMOND BEERS[229] 23 Sep 1956 in Norwich, Chenango Co., NY. He was born 24 Mar 1934.

Children of EDNA GOODRICH and EDWARD BEERS are:
     i. EDWARD RAYMOND[7] BEERS, JR., b. 22 Aug 1958; m. DONNA RENA DAY[230]; b. 1948.
77. ii. ANDREW CARLTON BEERS, b. 11 May 1960.

62. BRENDA[6] WARCUP *(JOHN F[5], GERTRUDE "GERTIE" E.[4] LECLAR, FERDINAND[3], JOHN BATTIS[2], ANTHONY[1])* She married MICHAEL KELLY.

Children of BRENDA WARCUP and MICHAEL KELLY are:
     i. ALLISON[7] KELLY.
     ii. COURTNEY KELLY.

63. ROBERT RAYMOND[6] RUHM, JR. *(RAYMOND ROBERT[5], MARY C.[4] BARNES, SARAH JANE[3] BUTLER, MARY ANN[2] LECLAR, ANTHONY[1])* was born 19 Jun 1919 in Utica, Oneida County, NY[231], and died 21 Jan 2009 in Utica, Oneida County, NY[231]. He married JANET P. ENGDAHL[232], daughter of EDWIN ENGDAHL and AGNES PAGEL. She was born Abt. 1920 in Minnesota, and died Jun 2003 in Utica, Oneida County, NY.

Obituary for JANE ENGDAHL (sister of JANET P. ENGDAHL):
Wednesday, March 28, 2007
Jane Marilyn Engdahl, 83, of New Hartford, died March 26, 2007 at the
Sitrin Healthcare Center. She was born February 27, 1924 in
Minneapolis, MN, daughter of the late Edwin and Agnes Pagel Engdahl.
She graduated from the University of Minneapolis, MN with a degree in
Library Science. She was of the Catholic faith. Despite her physical
limitations, Marilyn had a love of sports, traveling and spending time
with her family. She is survived by her brother-in-law, Robert Ruhm, Jr.
of Utica; her niece, Alison Jones and husband, Jack of New Hartford;
nephews, Robert Ruhm, III and wife, Maureen of Utica, Gordon Ruhm
of Utica; her great-nieces, Courtney and Kelly Jones of New Hartford.
She was predeceased by her sister, Janet Ruhm and her great-nephew,
Jack Price Jones, Jr. The family wishes to extend their thanks to the staff
of 40 West at Sitrin Healthcare for their many years of caring for
Marilyn. Private services will be held at the convenience of the family.
There are no calling hours. Interment will be in Crown Hill Memorial
Park. In lieu of flowers, kindly consider donations to United Cerebral
Palsy or Sitrin Healthcare in her memory. Arrangements are with the
Dimbleby, Friedel, Williams & Edmunds Funeral Home, 13 Oxford Rd.

Children of ROBERT RUHM and JANET ENGDAHL are:
78. i. ALISON[7] RUHM.
    ii. ROBERT RUHM III, b. Abt. 1946; m. MAUREEN LEVINE; b. Bet. 1950 - 1956.
   iii. GORDON K. RUHM.

64. GEORGE D.[6] GALLAGHER *(CHARLES F.[5], CHARLES RICHARD[4], MARTHA[3] MAHEDY, JANE[2] LECLAR, ANTHONY[1])* was born 03 Jan 1948 in Barre, Washington Co., VT, and died 1993 in Lebanon, NH. He married a MAZZINI and they had one child..

Generation No. 7

65. SUSAN[7] FEAR *(RUTH M.[6] DAVIS, HAROLD E.[5], CALIFERNA[4] LECLAR, FERDINAND[3], JOHN BATTIS[2], ANTHONY[1])* She married (1) RICHARD NORMAN. She married (2) AMBROSE MCDONALD.

Children of SUSAN FEAR and RICHARD NORMAN are:
  i. DAVID[8] NORMAN.
  ii. CRISTEEN NORMAN.

66. JOANN[7] WILLIAMS *(DOROTHEA L.[6] JONES, LULA M.[5] DAVIS, CALIFERNA[4] LECLAR, FERDINAND[3], JOHN BATTIS[2], ANTHONY[1])* was born 1952. She married WALTER TOMASIK. He was born 1951.

Child of JOANN WILLIAMS and WALTER TOMASIK is:
79. i. AMY[8] TOMASIK, b. 1972.

67. HOWARD[7] AUSTIN *(CHARLOTTE[6] JONES, LULA M.[5] DAVIS, CALIFERNA[4] LECLAR, FERDINAND[3], JOHN BATTIS[2], ANTHONY[1])*[233] was born 1956. He married (1) LINDA SNYDER. She was born 25 Oct 1948, and died 08 Oct 1990. He married (2) KELLIANN GUDS. She was born 1965.

Children of HOWARD AUSTIN and KELLIANN GUDS are:
  i. DAVID[8] AUSTIN, b. 1995.
  ii. DANIEL AUSTIN, b. 1998.

68. STEVEN[7] AUSTIN *(CHARLOTTE[6] JONES, LULA M.[5] DAVIS, CALIFERNA[4] LECLAR, FERDINAND[3], JOHN BATTIS[2], ANTHONY[1])* was born 1957. He married DEBRA LONDON[233]. She was born 1957.

91

Children of STEVEN AUSTIN and DEBRA LONDON are:
80.   i.   JENNIFER[8] AUSTIN, b. 1981.
       ii. AMY AUSTIN, b. 1984.

69. ANDREW[7] AUSTIN *(CHARLOTTE[6] JONES, LULA M.[5] DAVIS, CALIFERNA[4] LECLAR, FERDINAND[3], JOHN BATTIS[2], ANTHONY[1])* was born 1960. He married TERESA TETRAULT. She was born 1962.

Child of ANDREW AUSTIN and TERESA TETRAULT is:
       i.   ASHLEY[8] AUSTIN, b. 1986.

70. TIMOTHY[7] AUSTIN *(CHARLOTTE[6] JONES, LULA M.[5] DAVIS, CALIFERNA[4] LECLAR, FERDINAND[3], JOHN BATTIS[2], ANTHONY[1])* was born 1961. He married DIANA VEDDER. She was born 1963.

Children of TIMOTHY AUSTIN and DIANA VEDDER are:
       i.   COURTNEY[8] AUSTIN, b. 1985.
      ii. STEPHEN AUSTIN, b. 1989.

71. JULIE[7] AUSTIN *(CHARLOTTE[6] JONES, LULA M.[5] DAVIS, CALIFERNA[4] LECLAR, FERDINAND[3], JOHN BATTIS[2], ANTHONY[1])* was born 1964. She married TIM RUHREN. He was born 1966.

Children of JULIE AUSTIN and TIM RUHREN are:
       i.   ALEXANDER[8] RUHREN, b. 2000.
      ii. PETER RUHREN, b. 2002.

72. RODNEY ALBERT[7] NESTLE *(GRACE ELEANOR[6] LECLAR, JESSE FERDINAND[5], JOHN[4], FERDINAND[3], JOHN BATTIS[2], ANTHONY[1])* was born 28 Sep 1943 in Oneida County, NY. He married (1) GERALDINE MARIE DIXON[234] 20 Jul 1968[234], daughter of WALTER DIXON. She was born Abt. 1943. He married (2) PATRICIA E. WHITE BALL[234] 14 Jul 1984[234].

Child of RODNEY NESTLE and GERALDINE DIXON is:

    i.   RODNEY ALBERT[8] NESTLE, JR., b. 26 Nov 1969[234]; m. (1) JULIE, and then divorced; m. (2) DENISE M., 04 Jul 2002.

Harold Richard "Dick" and Joyce Beverly (Sage) LeClar

and their daughter, Susan Marie LeClar

73. HAROLD RICHARD "DICK"[7] LECLAR *(HAROLD JESSE[6], JESSE FERDINAND[5], JOHN[4], FERDINAND[3], JOHN BATTIS[2], ANTHONY[1])* was born 13 Sep 1942 in Rome, Oneida County, NY[234,235]. He married, 13 Jul 1963 in Oneida County, NY[236], JOYCE BEVERLY SAGE[235], daughter of LLOYD SAGE and FREDA BERGER. She was born 27 Mar 1943[237].

DICK was a civilian fire fighter at Griffith Air Force Base in Rome, NY. He is an active cattle rancher, raising American Highland Cattle. He was elected to the office of Vice President, American Highland Cattle Association and President of the Northeast Highland Cattle Association. DICK is also active as an auctioneer, partnering with his brother JERRY in The Gavel in Oxford, NY. He lives with his wife, JOYCE, in Boonville, Oneida County, NY

Children of HAROLD LECLAR and JOYCE SAGE are:
     i. SUSAN MARIE[9] LECLAR, b. 8 Oct 1968, Oneida County, NY.
    ii. SHARON LYNN LECLAR, b. 8 Oct 1968, Oneida County, NY; d. 9 Oct 1968, Oneida County, NY.

Gerald Allen "Jerry" & Geraldine K. "Gerry" (Zimmerman) LeClar

74. GERALD ALLEN "JERRY"[7] LECLAR *(HAROLD JESSE[6], JESSE FERDINAND[5], JOHN[4], FERDINAND[3], JOHN BATTIS[2], ANTHONY[1])* was born 08 Jun 1949 in Oneida County, NY. He married GERALDINE "GERRY" K. ZIMMERMAN 08 Nov 1975, daughter of DANIEL and DENISE ZIMMERMAN. She was born Dec 1948.

JERRY was an Agricultural Resource Specialist with Cornell University Cooperative Extension Service. After retiring he studied auctioneering and real estate and is currently a partner with his brother DICK in The Gavel, an auction house in Oxford, NY. He is a Past President of the New York State Auctioneers Association, a licensed Real Estate Salesman, and a farming Consultant. He lives with his wife, GERRY, in Oxford, NY.

Children of GERALD LECLAR and GERALDINE ZIMMERMAN are:

81.   i.   NADINE RENEE[8] LECLAR, b. 29 Dec 1977, New York.

       ii.   CHRISTOPHER TODD LECLAR, b. 24 Nov 1979, New York; m. PATRICIA MARTINEZ; b. 19 Nov 1973.

Photo overleaf

The Jerry & Gerry LeClar Family

left-to-right & top-to-bottom:

Patricia (Martinez) & Christopher Todd LeClar
Timothy & Nadine Renee (LeClar) Kneale
Jerry & Gerry LeClar
Pyper Makayla Kneale & Brandon Tyler Kneale

75. GARY W.[7] CUMMINGS *(CLAYTON LEON[6], FLORENCE E.[5] LECLAR, JOHN[4], FERDINAND[3], JOHN BATTIS[2], ANTHONY[1])* was born 09 Oct 1945[240]. He married CAROL QUINN[240] 20 Jun 1970[240], daughter of WILLIAM QUINN. She was born Abt. 1945.

GARY worked at the Utica State Hospital and the New York Psychiatric Center for 23 years[241]

CAROL worked at Marcy State Hosptital and the Mohawk Valley Psychiatric Center for 38 years[241]

Children of GARY CUMMINGS and CAROL QUINN are:

82.　　i.　KATHY[8] CUMMINGS, b. 02 Nov 1971.
83.　　ii.　LANCE CUMMINGS, b. 16 Nov 1973.

76. JAMES WILLIAM[7] LAWRENCE *(JOYCE MARIE[6] GOODRICH, NELLIE HOGAN[5] LECLAR, JOHN[4], FERDINAND[3], JOHN BATTIS[2], ANTHONY[1])*[243] was born 13 Oct 1951 in Norwich, Chenango County, New York. He married (1) MARY KATHRINE THERESA CAMPBELL Abt. 1975. She was born 1951. He married (2) LINDA KAY FINE. She was born 1945.

JAMES served in the U.S. Army as a Sgt.

Children of JAMES LAWRENCE and MARY CAMPBELL are:

　　　　i.　ALEXANDER JOSEPH[8] LAWRENCE, b. 1976; md. BRANDI LEANN NICHOLS; b. 1983.
84.　　ii.　JESSICA-JAMIE KATHLEEN LAWRENCE, b. 1978.

77. ANDREW CARLTON[7] BEERS *(EDNA BELLE[6] GOODRICH, NELLIE HOGAN[5] LECLAR, JOHN[4], FERDINAND[3], JOHN BATTIS[2], ANTHONY[1])* was born 11 May 1960. He married ELIZABETH EDITH MEER. She was born 1958.

Children of ANDREW BEERS and ELIZABETH MEER are:

　　　　i.　AUGUST DEFORD[8] BEERS[244], b. 1994.
　　　　ii.　ALTHEA PHILAMEN BEERS[244].

78. ALISON[7] RUHM *(ROBERT RAYMOND[6], RAYMOND ROBERT[5], MARY C.[4] BARNES, SARAH JANE[3] BUTLER, MARY ANN[2] LECLAR, ANTHONY[1])* She married JACK PRICE JONES.

Children of ALISON RUHM and JACK JONES are:
    i.   COURTNEY[8] JONES.
   ii.   KELLY JONES.
  iii.   JACK PRICE JONES, JR., d. Bef. 28 Mar 2007.

Generation No. 8

79. AMY[8] TOMASIK *(JOANN[7] WILLIAMS, DOROTHEA L.[6] JONES, LULA M.[5] DAVIS, CALIFERNA[4] LECLAR, FERDINAND[3], JOHN BATTIS[2], ANTHONY[1])* was born 1972.

Child of AMY TOMASIK is:
    i.   MATTHEW[9], b. 1994.

80. JENNIFER[8] AUSTIN *(STEVEN[7], CHARLOTTE[6] JONES, LULA M.[5] DAVIS, CALIFERNA[4] LECLAR, FERDINAND[3], JOHN BATTIS[2], ANTHONY[1])* was born 1981. She married RANDY THOMAS.

Child of JENNIFER AUSTIN and RANDY THOMAS is:
    i.   AUSTIN[9] THOMAS, b. 2006.

81. NADINE RENEE[8] LECLAR *(GERALD ALLEN "JERRY"[7], HAROLD JESSE[6], JESSE FERDINAND[5], JOHN[4], FERDINAND[3], JOHN BATTIS[2], ANTHONY[1])*[245] was born 29 Dec 1977 in New York[245]. She married, 20 Jul 2003[245], TIMOTHY KNEALE[245]. He was born 13 Jan 1980[245].

Children of NADINE LECLAR and TIMOTHY KNEALE are:
    i.   BRANDON TYLER[9] KNEALE[245], b. 26 Feb 2003, New York[245].
    ii. PYPER MAKAYLA KNEALE[245], b. 05 Apr 2005, New York[245].

82. KATHY[8] CUMMINGS *(GARY W.[7], CLAYTON LEON[6], FLORENCE E.[5] LECLAR, JOHN[4], FERDINAND[3], JOHN BATTIS[2], ANTHONY[1])*[246] was born 02 Nov 1971[246]. She married ADAM BECKERMAN[246]. He was born Abt. 1970.

Children of KATHY CUMMINGS and ADAM BECKERMAN are:
    i.   MAX[9] BECKERMAN, b. 2001.
    ii. SAM BECKERMAN, b. 2004.

83. LANCE[8] CUMMINGS *(GARY W.[7], CLAYTON LEON[6], FLORENCE E.[5] LECLAR, JOHN[4], FERDINAND[3], JOHN BATTIS[2], ANTHONY[1])[246]* was born 16 Nov 1973[246]. He married MELISSA STRIFE. She was born Abt. 1973.

Children of LANCE CUMMINGS and MELISSA STRIFE are:
     i.   MICHAEL[9] CUMMINGS, b. 2001.
    ii.   MARGARET CUMMINGS, b. 2005.

84. JESSICA-JAMIE KATHLEEN[8] LAWRENCE *(JAMES WILLIAM[7], JOYCE MARIE[6] GOODRICH, NELLIE HOGAN[5] LECLAR, JOHN[4], FERDINAND[3], JOHN BATTIS[2], ANTHONY[1])* was born 1978. She married JOSEPH WYLIE ELSHEIMER. He was born 1977.

Children of JESSICA-JAMIE LAWRENCE and JOSEPH ELSHEIMER are:
     i.   AUSTIN THOMAS[9] ELSHEIMER, b. 1997.
    ii.   MICHAEL SCOTT ELSHEIMER, b. 1999.
   iii.   ANTHONY DAL-LEON ELSHEIMER, b. 2001.

Index of Individuals

Surname -
Given Name   Page No.

Index of Individuals

Elizabeth: 48
A. -
Gertrude: 71
Anderson -
Lena B.: 67
Angus -
Stella: 73, 74
Austin -
Amy: 92
Andrew: 76, 92
Ashley: 92
Courtney: 92
Daniel: 91
David: 91
Howard: 76, 91
Howard D.: 76
Jennifer: 92, 101
Julie: 76, 92
Stephen: 92
Steven: 76, 91, 92
Timothy: 76, 92
Avard -
Jesse: 50
Marion: 50
Ball -
Patricia E. White: 92
Ballou -
Arthur (1887): 47
Arthur (1912): 47
Barnes -
Adin P.: 23
Alfred: 23
Lillie: 23
Mary C.: 23, 24
Richard: 23
Richard D.: 213
Robert: 23
Barrett -
Melissa Marie: 89   103

Beckerman -
    Adam: 101
    Max: 101
    Sam: 101
Beers -
    Althea Philamen: 99
    Andrew Carlton: 89, 99
    August Deford: 99
    Edward Raymond: 89
    Edward Raymond , Jr.: 89
Benedict -
    Ralph Babbitt: 72
    Virginia: 72
Berger -
    Freda: 95
Brement -
    Bruce: 68
Brown -
    Eloise: 70
    Walter M.: 70
Burch -
    Elba A.: 59
Butler -
    Adin H.: 7
    Alfred: 7
    Barbara: 44
    Child: 21
    Flera M.: 21
    Joseph: 7
    Joseph Milton: 23, 43, 44
    Milton G.: 21
    Sarah Jane: 8, 23
    Shirley: 44
    Solomon: 23
    Tina: 21
    Zora Winifred: 23
Campbell -
    Mary Kathrine Theresa: 99
Cavanaugh -
    Alice J.: 59, 65
    George: 59
Chandler -
    Anna: 59
Clamp -
    Two Children: 74
    Ronald: 74

Coburn -
  Albert: 24
  Alfred: 24
  Emily J.: 24
  Flora M.: 24
  Michael: 24
  Sarah G.: 24
  William: 24
Corr -
  Eleanor A.: 68
  William J.: 68
Cummings -
  Carlisle: 88
  Clarence W.: 65
  Clayton Leon: 60, 87, 88
  Doris Marjorie: 60, 61
  Gary W.: 88, 99
  Harley C.: 65, 88
  James John "Pete": 62 - 65
  Kathy: 99, 101
  Lance: 99, 102
  Leon James: 59, 60, 65
  Margaret: 102
  Michael: 102
  Walter J.: 59
Davis -
  Betty E.: 53
  Carl: 51
  Catherine: 29
  Edward: 29
  Grace: 57
  Harold E.: 30, 53
  Howard L.: 50
  Hugh R.: 29, 30
  Leroy F.: 30, 50
  Lloyd H.: 30
  Lula M.: 30, 55
  Lyndon Garry: 51
  Marjorie E.: 53, 76
  Mildred G.: 53, 75
  Ruth M.: 53, 75
  Velma: 51
  Willard: 53
Day -
  Donna Rena: 89
Dewitt -
  Child: 49
  Unknown: 49

Dewitt -
    Geraldine Marie: 49
    Walter: 49
Douglass -
    Elizabeth: 5
Downs -
    Clayton J.: 27, 48
    Jack: 48
    Joseph: 26, 27
    Margaret Mary Bridget: 27
    Martha: 27
    Mary "Minnie": 25
    Mary Ellen "Nellie": 27
    Mary Madeline: 27, 49
    Mary Martha: 27
    Philip A.: 27
    Walter Edward: 27
E. -
    Olive: 50
Edwards -
    Francis Myrtle Babe: 21
    Reuben David: 21
Ellis -
    Jane: 87
Elsheimer -
    Anthony Dal-Leon: 102
    Austin Thomas: 102
    Joseph Wylie: 102
    Michael Scott: 102
Engdahl -
    Edwin: 89
    Janet P.: 89
Evans -
    Ethel E.: 87, 88
    John E.: 87
Farmer -
    Florence Parsons: 30
Fear -
    Norman: 75
    Steve: 75
    Susan: 75, 91
Felice -
    Joseph P.: 72
Fine -
    Linda Kay: 99

Gibbs -
Robert Flint: 71
Dr. Robert Flint D.: 39, 71
Romaine Delmont: 38, 39
Gillett -
Esther: 23
Goodfellow -
Anna: 39
Goodrich -
Edna Belle: 68, 69
James Vernon: 67
James Vernon , Jr.: 67, 68
Joyce Marie: 68, 88
Grabner -
Margaret "Maggie": 79
Grems -
Martha: 20
Griffin -
Maude A.: 48
Guds -
Kelliann: 91
Guilfoyle -
Elizabeth: 48
Frank B.: 26
James: 48
Leo Raymond: 48
Leona E.: 48, 74
Marjorie A.: 48, 74
Mary F.: 48, 74
Harper -
Michael: 11
Harrington -
Cynthia O.: 37
Haslock -
Dorothy E.: 71
Haynes -
Blanche: 71
Martha: 1
Herter -
Clarence M.: 76
Hill -
Ruby L.: 83
Hogan -
Michael: 33
Nellie R.: 33, 34
Sarah J.: 33

LeClar -
Anthony: 1
Asa Webster: 5
Califerna: 16, 29, 30
Christopher Todd: 97
Elizabeth: 6, 19
Ferdinand: 6, 15
Florence E.: 35, 59, 60
Floretta Louisa: 6
Gerald Allen "Jerry": 85, 97
Gertrude "Gertie" E.: 16, 37, 38
Grace Eleanor: 59, 79, 80
Harold Jesse: 59, 83, 85
Harold Richard "Dick": 85, 95
James Walker: 21
Jane: 2, 11
Jesse Ferdinand: 34, 35, 57, 59
Jessie Battes: 20
John: 16, 33, 34
John Battis: 1, 5
Dr. Leo Cowling: 21
Mabel G.: 35
Mary Ann (1816): 2, 7
Mary Ann (1839): 6, 19
Moulton: 2
Nadine Renee: 97, 101
Nellie Hogan: 35, 67, 68
Peter (1814): 2
Peter (1864): 16
Peter B. (1849): 6, 20
Sarah: 2, 8
Sharon Lynn: 95
Susan Marie: 95
Laquay -
Barbara: 88
Lefebre -
Olive: 73
Levine -
Maureen: 90
Lewis -
William E.: 57
Winifred H.: 57, 59
London -
Debra: 91, 92
M. -
Denise: 97
Jennie: 21

110

Mahedy -
Arthur: 26
Charles Anthony: 12
Cora A.: 26
Edward: 26
Elizabeth Jane: 11, 25
Ellen A.: 11
Ernest: 26
Esther A.: 23
James: 26
James Alfred: 12, 26
John Baptiste: 11
Marie Emacula: 12
Martha: 11, 25
Mary Ann: 12
Mary E.: 26, 48
Mary Jane "Jennie": 12, 26, 27
Michael: 23
Patrick: 11
Peter John: 11
Sarah Jane: 11, 24
Stephen Philip: 12
Marchand -
Ida: 43
Martin -
Frederick: 44
Martinez -
Patricia: 97
Mazzini -
Unknown: 90
McCaffrey -
Charles: 25
Elizabeth: 25
Henry: 25
Margarite: 25
McDonald -
Ambrose: 75
Ambrose: 91
Annie: 62, 64, 65
James: 12
McNeil -
John: 25
John: 25
Peter: 25
Meeker -
Audra Minnie: 83, 85
Jerry C.: 83

Descendants of Francois Leclercq

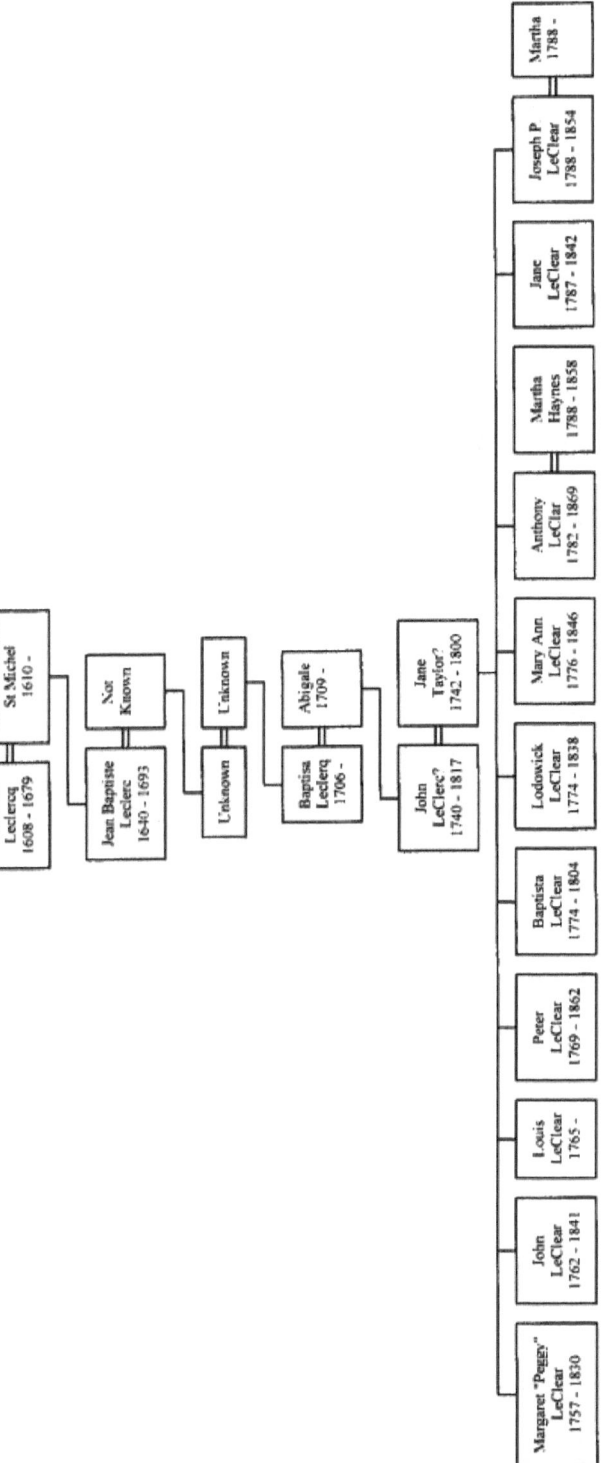

1. findagrave.com, Martha Haynes LeClar data, Tombstone inscription: wife of Anthony Leclar, age 69 yrs 10 mos..
2. findagrave.com, Tombstone inscription.
3. 1850 Federal Census.
4. Rome Sentinel, July 16, 1885.
5. findagrave.com, Tombstone inscription.
6. 1880 California Federal Census.
7. 1880 Federal Census.
8. 1860 Federal Census.
9. findagrave.com, Gravestone inscription.
10. 1900 Federal Census.
11. Rome Sentinel, Feb 8/9 1908.
12. findagrave.com, John Battis LeClar data, Tombstone Inscription: Died: Jan 30, 1864age: 55 yrs 8 mos 9 dys.
13. findagrave.com, John Battis LeClar data.
14. Gravestone record, Gravestone says: Floretta .
15. Gravestone record, died: Jan 15, 1883, aged 35 years.
16. Rome Citizen, July 11, 1895.
17. 1900 Federal Census.
18. Obituary.
19. Gravestone record.
20. Obituary.
21. Gravestone record.
22. Obituary.
23. Gravestone record.
24. Obituary.
25. 1900 Federal Census.
26. findagrave.com.
27. Gravestone record.
28. 1900 Federal Census.
29. findagrave.com.
30. Obituary.
31. 1900 Federal Census.
32. Rome Sentinel, Dec 10, 1925.
33. Obituary.
34. findagrave.com.
35. 1900 Federal Census.
36. findagrave.com.
37. 1900 Federal Census.
38. 1880 Federal Census.
39. findagrave.com.
40. 1900 Federal Census.
41. 1880 Federal Census.
42. 1900 Federal Census.
43. findagrave.com.

44. 1850 Federal Census, Peter LeClar, age: 0 (so must have been born in early 1850 or late 1849.
45. Ohio Death Certificate Index.
46. 1880 Federal Census.
47. 1900 Federal Census.
48. Ohio Deaths 1908-1953, Family Search.
49. Ohio Obituary Index, 1830-2009.
50. Ohio Deaths 1908-1953.
51. 1900 Federal Census.
52. WWII Draft registration card.
53. WWI Draft registration card.
54. 1920 Federal Census.
55. WWI Draft registration card.
56. Montana Death Index.
57. Ancestry.com Kelly Pease family tree.
58. Directory of Deceased American Physicians, 1804-1929.
59. WWI Draft registration card.
60. Ancestry.com Kelly Pease family tree.
61. 1900 Federal Census.
62. 1880 Federal Census.
63. 1900 Federal Census.
64. 1880 Federal Census.
65. Audra LeClar manuscripts.
66. 1900 Federal Census.
67. Ancestry.com Public family pages, Janet's Mahady / Mahedy Clan.
68. findagrave.com.
69. Gravestone record.
70. findagrave.com.
71. Gravestone record.
72. findagrave.com.
73. Gravestone record.
74. findagrave.com.
75. Gravestone record.
76. findagrave.com.
77. 1870 Federal Census.
78. findagrave.com.
79. Gravestone record.
80. findagrave.com.
81. SSDI.
82. 1930 Federal Census.
83. Gravestone record.
84. findagrave.com.
85. Gravestone record.
86. WWI Draft registration card.
87. Death Certificate.
88. WWI Draft registration card.
89. 1930 Federal Census.
90. 1900 Federal Census.

91. 1920 Federal Census.
92. 1900 Federal Census.
93. Audra LeClar manuscripts.
94. 1900 Federal Census.
95. http://newsarch.rootsweb.com/th/read/QUEBEC-RESEARCH/2008-06/1212796243.
96. Audra LeClar manuscripts.
97. 1900 Federal Census.
98. Obituary for John LeClar.
99. Audra LeClar manuscripts.
100. 1900 Federal Census.
101. findagrave.com.
102. Audra LeClar manuscripts, Obituary for Gertie Warcup.
103. Audra LeClar manuscripts.
104. WWI Draft registration card.
105. findagrave.com.
106. Audra LeClar manuscripts, Obituary for Frank Warcup.
107. Audra LeClar manuscripts.
108. SSDI.
109. Audra LeClar manuscripts, Obituary for Harold Warcup.
110. findagrave.com.
111. SSDI.
112. Audra LeClar manuscripts, Obituary for Harold Warcup.
113. 1880 Federal Census.
114. 1900 Federal Census.
115. 1860 Federal Census, Ava, Oneida County, NY, age 10/12 yrs (ie. 10 months old).
116. 1850 Federal Census.
117. 1900 Federal Census.
118. 1870 Federal Census.
119. 1910 Federal Census.
120. 1900 Federal Census.
121. Rootsweb/Ancestry Family Trees, Kenneth W. Flint Family.
122. 1880 Federal Census.
123. findagrave.com.
124. Newspaper clipping.
125. 1900 Federal Census.
126. Newspaper clipping, March 8, 1940 ... Mortimer W. Flint died Thursday night.
127. Newspaper clipping.
128. 1900 Federal Census.
129. Newspaper clipping.
130. SSDI.
131. findagrave.com.
132. WWI Draft registration card.
133. Bernice's Obit.
134. 1870 Federal Census.
135. 1870 Federal Census, Lewis County, NY, 7/12 yrs old.

136. findagrave.com.
137. 1900 Federal Census.
138. SSDI.
139. 1880 Federal Census, Living with g-parents, Charles and.Sarah (LeClar) Reynolds
140. 1900 Federal Census.
141. 1910 Federal Census.
142. WWII Draft registration card.
143. WWI Draft registration card.
144. WWII Draft registration card.
145. WWI Draft registration card.
146. WWII Draft registration card.
147. 1930 Federal Census.
148. WWI Draft registration card.
149. WWII Draft registration card.
150. 1930 Federal Census.
151. 1900 Federal Census.
152. 1920 Federal Census, age 3 yrs, 3 moCensus date of Jan 1, 1920.
153. 1920 Federal Census, age 6 mo.Census date of Jan 1, 1920.
154. 1930 Federal Census.
155. 1900 Federal Census.
156. Audra LeClar manuscripts.
157. 1930 Federal Census.
158. 1920 Federal Census.
159. 1930 Federal Census.
160. 1900 Federal Census.
161. Audra LeClar manuscripts.
162. 1930 Federal Census.
163. Audra LeClar manuscripts.
164. Jerry LeClar.
165. 1920 Federal Census.
166. 1930 Federal Census.
167. Jerry LeClar.
168. SSDI.
169. Audra LeClar manuscripts, Wedding anniversary announcements.
170. 1910 Federal Census.
171. Audra LeClar manuscripts, Obituary for Leon Cummings.
172. 1900 Federal Census.
173. Audra LeClar manuscripts, Obituary for Leon Cummings.
174. WWI Draft registration card.
175. 1910 Federal Census.
176. Audra LeClar manuscripts, Obituary for Leon Cummings.
177. Audra LeClar manuscripts.
178. Gravestone record.
179. Obituary.
180. Audra LeClar manuscripts, Wedding notice.
181. SSDI.
182. Obituary for Nellie R. LeClar.

183. 1930 Federal Census.
184. SSDI.
185. findagrave.com.
186. Audra LeClar manuscripts, Obituary for Harold Warcup.
187. SSDI.
188. 1900 Federal Census.
189. WWI Draft registration card.
190. SSDI.
191. 1920 Federal Census.
192. New York Passenger Lists, 1820-1957, 1954 > June > 15 > Queen Elizabeth.
193. 1900 Federal Census.
194. SSDI.
195. 1930 Federal Census.
196. SSDI.
197. WWI Draft registration card.
198. IGI.
199. SSDI.
200. findagrave.com.
201. 1910 Federal Census.
202. findagrave.com.
203. Gravestone record.
204. SSDI.
205. 1930 Federal Census.
206. 1920 Federal Census, age 1 yr 8 months.
207. 1930 Federal Census.
208. SSDI.
209. Marjorie Herter obit.
210. Daniel Sexton obit.
211. Audra LeClar manuscripts.
212. 1930 Federal Census.
213. SSDI.
214. Audra LeClar manuscripts.
215. SSDI.
216. Rome Sentinel.
217. Gravestone record.
218. SSDI.
219. Audra LeClar manuscripts.
220. SSDI.
221. Winnifred Lewis LeClar Obituary.
222. Audra LeClar manuscripts.223. SSDI.
224. Audra LeClar manuscripts.
225. SSDI.
226. Audra LeClar manuscripts.
227. Audra LeClar manuscripts, Obituary for Nellie Goodrich.
228. Whitepages.com.
229. Audra LeClar manuscripts, Obituary for Nellie Goodrich.
230. Linda Kay Lawrence.

231. SSDI.
232. Jane Engdahl obituary.
233. Pete Cummings.
234. Audra LeClar manuscripts.
235. Dick LeClar.
236. Audra LeClar manuscripts.
237. Dick LeClar.
238. Audra LeClar manuscripts.
239. Jerry LeClar.
240. Audra LeClar manuscripts.
241. Linda Kay Lawrence.
242. Audra LeClar manuscripts.
243. Audra LeClar manuscripts, Obituary for Nellie Goodrich.
244. Linda Kay Lawrence.
245. Jerry LeClar.
246. Audra LeClar manuscripts.